Advance Praise for
Student Success in Higher Education

The authors of *Student Success in Higher Education* have constructed a model that provides strategies for academic advisors, career and personal counselors, faculty, and student engagement specialists—all of whom assume some role in fostering student success in college students—to be successful in that role themselves. The model is based upon using each student's own internal self-knowledge, understanding, goals, values, and resources in determining his/her own criteria for success.

Elaine and Henry Brzycki have explored and presented relevant research that supports the standards of various professional associations that advocate for student success, and they offer a collaborative model that enables student success professionals to focus their work on what our college students identify as their own successes.

Depending on one's perspective, the three high-impact practices used in the model can both minimize and maximize the emphasis on the primary single criterion of degree completion, which has become the de facto definition of student success. Students who are aware of and supported in their personal selves will be able to define what success means for them and to confront external conditions more readily in order to strive to meet their own criteria. In doing so, they will more likely to meet the completion criterion as well. It really is a win-win situation.

Thomas J. Grites, PhD
Assistant Provost
Stockton University
Past National Academic Advising Association (NACADA) president
and higher education thought leader

Dr. Brzycki's novel concept of the *iSelf* uses 21st-century terminology for terms earlier introduced to convey less comprehensive concepts such as soul, reality-oriented ego, and mind. However, his *iSelf* emerges from the interaction of current scientific information about the direct influence by emotions, both positive and negative, upon cognitive functioning. These emotions, in turn, are based upon personal relevancy and meaningfulness and are the controlling switch by which effective learning takes place or not. A positive emotional approach facilitates a sense of well-being that, in turn, enhances a willingness to learn. The outcome, in turn, promotes a greater sense of well-being and less reason for persons to engage in self-destructive behaviors.

Frederick M. Brown, PhD
Associate Professor and Director, Human Performance Rhythms Laboratory
The Pennsylvania State University—University Park
Department of Psychology—Cognitive and Wellness
Psychology of well-being researcher and author of Positive Psychology and Well Being: Applications for Enhanced Living *(with Dr. Cynthia LaJambe), 2016*

Student Success in Higher Education tackles some of the most salient issues of our time. Most notably, the text attempts to answer the following question throughout: How can we successfully balance students' well-being with holistic learning and the rigor associated with postsecondary education? Referencing national and international higher education organizations, along with previous research on student success, the text will certainly stimulate new ways of approaching high-impact practices. *Student Success in Higher Education* is a necessary text for anyone that works directly with college students, but essential for support services within academic and student affairs.

Matthew Shupp, EdD
Assistant Professor and Coordinator, College Counseling /
College Student Personnel Specializations
Department of Counseling and College Student Personnel
Shippensburg University

College students' well-being is central to their ability to accomplish their personal and academic goals, and yet can be easily neglected with the increasingly fast paced, demanding, and social media driven lives that they experience. *Student Success in Higher Education* draws on research and best practice examples to demonstrate how to promote well-being across key academic and student affairs areas. The book describes an appealing student centered model that stems from a positive psychology perspective, and focuses on effective practices for fostering student success.

Larry Marks, PhD
Licensed Psychologist
University of Central Florida, Counseling and Psychological Services
Co-editor of Positive Psychology on the College Campus (2015)

The national conversation on higher education has moved from a focus primarily on access (everyone can get in somewhere) to one of completion (earning a credential). This shift is welcome, but insufficient. Student affairs is uniquely poised to promote not only student completion, but also student success. In this context that means growth, development, maturation, and learning. This book will help student affairs educators ensure that students are getting the experiences they need to graduate from college and thrive in life.

Case Willoughby, EdD
Vice President for Student Affairs and Enrollment Management
Butler County Community College

STUDENT SUCCESS IN HIGHER EDUCATION

STUDENT SUCCESS IN HIGHER EDUCATION

Developing the Whole Person through High-Impact Practices

Elaine J. Brzycki and Henry G. Brzycki

Copyright © 2016 by Elaine J. Brzycki and Henry G. Brzycki.

All rights reserved.

Printed in the United States of America. No part of this book may be used or reproduced in any manner without written permission except in the case of brief quotations embodied in critical articles and reviews, and in scholarly research. For information, contact Dr. Henry G. Brzycki, 2352 Park Center Boulevard, State College, PA 16801, or Henry@Brzyckigroup.com.

This publication is designed to provide accurate and authoritative information in regard to the subject matter covered. It is sold with the understanding that the author and publisher are not engaged in rendering legal, accounting, psychological, medical, or other professional service. If expert assistance is required, the services of a competent professional person should be sought.

Cover and interior design by Rachel Paul, Lotus Editing and Design, Philadelphia, PA.

Library of Congress Cataloging-in-Publication Data
Elaine J. Brzycki and Henry G. Brzycki, Student Success in Higher Education:
Developing the Whole Person through High-Impact Practices

Includes bibliographical references and index.
ISBNs: 978-0-9887161-5-5 (paper); 978-0-9887161-4-8 (Nook); 978-0-9887161-6-2 (Kindle); 978-0-9887161-7-9 (PDF)

Counseling and Psychological Services, Academic Advising, Faculty teaching and learning.
2. Psychological and physical well-being.

I. Title.
LCCN: 2016909470
Imprint Name: BG Publishing, State College, PA
Printed in the United States of America

To each other

The following colleges and universities are referenced throughout this book:

American Public University
Arkansas Technical University
Brown University
Bryant University
Butler County Community College
California State University System
Clarion University of Pennsylvania
Cornell University
Emporia State University
Florida State University
Harvard University
High Point University
Minnesota State Colleges and Universities System
Ohio State University
Pennsylvania State University
Shippensburg University of Pennsylvania
St. Petersburg College
Stockton University
University of Central Florida
University of Florida
University of Michigan
University of Pennsylvania
Wright State University

The following professional organizations are referenced throughout this book:

American College Personnel Association (ACPA)
Association of American Colleges and Universities (AAC&U)
Carnegie Foundation for Teaching
Community College Survey of Student Engagement (CCSSE)
Council for the Advancement of Standards (CAS)
Faculty Survey of Student Engagement (FSSE)
International Association of Counseling Services (IACS)
National Academic Advising Association (NACADA)
National Association of Colleges and Employers (NACE)
National Association of Student Personnel Administrators (NASPA)
National Career Development Association (NCDA)
National Survey of Student Engagement (NSSE)

Please see the index for specific page references.

Contents

Preface		xv
Acknowledgments		xxi
Chapter 1	Higher Education and the Decline of Well-Being	1
	Students and Dissonance	3
	Student Concerns	6
	College Students Are Not Well	6
	Well-Being in the United States	7
	Long before They Arrive on Campus	8
	Anxiety and Loneliness	9
	Sexual Violence on Campus	10
	Depression	12
	Suicide	12
	Physical Health	13
	Demands of a Complex World	15
	Students' Changing Needs	15
	Completion Rates	16
	Internal versus External Selves	19
	Final Thoughts	21
Chapter 2	Student Success Redefined	23
	Student Success Requires Well-Being	23
	An Expanded Definition of Well-Being	24
	Self-Knowledge	26
	Student-Centered Education	29
	Learning through the Lens of the Self	30
	Final Thoughts	31
Chapter 3	Higher Education's New Mission	33
	Integrating Well-Being into Student Success Functions	33
	Feeling Engaged	34

	Student Success Activities	36
	Students' Personal Definitions of Success	37
	Integrated and Interdisciplinary	38
	Trends toward Integration	39
	Promoting Resilience	40
	Student Success Centers	41
	First-Year Programs	42
	High Stakes	43
	The Gap between Prevention and Treatment	44
	Gap between Mission and Practice	49
	Implications	50
	Final Thoughts	51
Chapter 4	Student Success and Professional Standards	55
	High-Impact Educational Practices	56
	ACPA and NASPA Student Success Standards	58
	Advising and Helping	59
	Student Learning and Development	61
	Personal Foundations	62
	NACADA Student Success Standards	64
	Core Value 1: Advisors Are Responsible to the Individuals They Advise	64
	Core Value 2: Advisors Are Responsible for Involving Others, When Appropriate, in the Advising Process	65
	Core Value 3: Advisors Are Responsible to Their Institutions	66
	Core Value 4: Advisors Are Responsible to Higher Education in General	66
	CAS Student Success Standards	66
	Student Learning and Development Domains and Dimensions	67
	IACS Student Success Standards	68
	Counseling Services Roles and Functions	69
	Individual and Group Counseling	69
	NCDA Student Success Standards	70
	Personal Social Development Domain	71
	Educational Achievement and Lifelong Learning Domain	71
	NACE Student Success Standards	72
	AAC&U Essential Learning Outcomes	73
	Knowledge of Human Cultures and the Physical and Natural World	73
	Intellectual and Practical Skills	74
	Personal and Social Responsibility	74
	Integrative and Applied Learning	74
	Final Thoughts	75

Chapter 5	Student Success High-Impact Practices	77
	Student Transformation	78
	Using Self-Knowledge to Make a Difference	79
	The Importance of Self-Knowledge	81
	Emotions and Cognition	82
	Integrated Self Model (*iSelf*)	83
	The Whole Person	84
	Self-System Attributes Defined	85
	Self-Concept	86
	Self-Esteem	86
	Self-Efficacy	87
	Self-Understanding	87
	Identity	88
	Locus of Control	89
	Self-Schema	89
	Self-Affect	90
	Positive Psychology Attributes	90
	Life Purpose and Spirituality	91
	Life Meaning	92
	Intrinsic Motivation	92
	Happiness	92
	Inspiration, Hope, and Dreams	93
	Possible Selves	94
	Self-Determination	94
	Emotional Intelligence and Positive Emotions	94
	Well-Being	95
	Creativity	95
	iSelf Implementation	96
	Developmental and Intrusive Advising	96
	Coaching	97
	Strengths-Based Counseling and Appreciative Inquiry	98
	Self Across the Curriculum (*SAC*)	101
	Connecting Academic Content to the Self	102
	SAC Helps Achieve NSSE and FSSE Results	104
	Faculty Learning about Mental Health and Well-Being	106
	Student-Centered Personalized Learning	107
	The *Success Predictor* (*SP*): For Academic, Career, and Life Direction	108
	Handbook for Administering the *Success Predictor*	109
	Instructions for Advisors, Counselors, and Faculty	110
	Questions to Support Your Inquiry	110
	Quotes to Support Your Inquiry	110

		Instructions for Students	111
		Categories	113
		Review and Analysis	113
		Suggestions for Advisors, Counselors, and Faculty	114
		How the *Success Predictor* Works	114
		Final Thoughts	117
Chapter 6		Student Success in Practice	119
		Teaching	120
		Promising Practice: Fostering Self-Direction through First-Year Seminars	120
		Promising Practice: Student Success Course	123
		High-Impact Practice: Teaching with *Self Across the Curriculum*	127
		High-Impact Practice: Enhancing Human Development Courses with the *iSelf* Model	129
		Academic Advising	131
		Promising Practice: Workshop Series on Student Success Dimensions	133
		Promising Practice: Individualized Student Learning Plans	134
		Promising Practice: Online Assessments	135
		Career Counseling	136
		Promising Practice: Integrating Career and Academic Advising	136
		Promising Practice: Designing Your Life Course	137
		High-Impact Practice: Aligning Life Purpose and Career Using the *Success Predictor*	138
		High-Impact Practice: Summer Bridge Program Using the *iSelf* Model	138
		High-Impact Practice: Integrating Career Counseling and Internships Using the *iSuccess* Model	140
		Counseling and Psychological Services (CAPS)	142
		Promising Practice: Focus on Life Purpose	142
		Promising Practice: Life Coaching and Student Success Coaching	142
		Promising Practice: Online Therapy	143
		Promising Practice: Student Wellness across the University	144
		High-Impact Practice: Well-Being Workshops Using the *iSelf* Model	145
		Student Engagement	146
		Promising Practice: Community Engagement	146
		Promising Practice: The Engaged University	146
		High-Impact Practice: Integrating Student Engagement through University Themes	148

Integration through Technology	150
Final Thoughts	151

Final Thoughts 155

Suggestions for . . .	155
Students	155
Faculty	156
Student Success Professionals	156
Institutions of Higher Education	157
Professional Organizations	157
Personal Reflections	158
Our Journey	159

References and Electronic Resources	161
Index	173
About the Authors	185
Related Resources from The Brzycki Group and	
The Center for the Self in Schools	187

Preface

College students are attempting to put together their worlds, realities, and pathways to success. Frontline educators, counselors, and advisors who support college and university students are looking for ways to help students create these pathways.

In this book, we put forth a new student success model that is based on the latest research in the psychology of well-being and student-centered learning. We provide methods for integrating five critical student success functional areas—academic advising, career services, counseling and psychological services (CAPS), faculty teaching, and student engagement. And we convey high-impact practices that will help students create their own pathways to success and determine their own metrics of success.

It is our highest hope, and an overarching theme throughout this book, that our readers will be able to step outside of their usual ways of thinking about student success and the well-being of our students and reevaluate the systems that we have in place to support them in living a happy, healthy, and flourishing life.

Higher Education Can Impact the Greater Good

People are naturally good and want to express what is unique to them and what they were born to be and do to impact the quality of life toward the greater good—for self, others, and all.

Psychologist Dacher Keltner (2009) makes the case, based on research in psychology, sociology, and neuroscience, that people are wired for good. More specifically, he looked at the science of emotions and how positive emotions such as love, compassion, and gratitude are contagious—and help bring out the good not only in ourselves but in others as well. "The origins of human goodness...are rooted in our emotion, and these social instincts may be stronger than those of any other instinct or motive" (p. 73).

We believe that education should act for the greater good and facilitate and empower students in their quest for the greater good. It is important to think about the greater good for humanity in terms of the quality of our existence as a people and as individuals. Here we can intertwine the development of society's institutions with the networks of support that sustain the individual's development, resulting in the expansion of our human consciousness—our awareness of ourselves and what is possible.

The greater good is the idea that one ought to perform those actions that produce the greatest positive outcomes for the greatest numbers, and it is important for educators to consider themselves as trustees of the human condition. When making public policy or organizational decisions, the outcome or result demonstrates whether or not the action is justified. If methods exist to empower college-aged adolescents and young adults to create a positive life course trajectory by transforming the quality of their college experiences and lives, we as educators have the moral obligation to make these methods available to them.

Well-Being and Self-Knowledge

We believe that there is an inherent, basic, instinctual knowing about what is good for oneself and for others—and that is a life for everyone filled with *well-being*. Further, our research has found that people cannot be well if they do not have self-knowledge. Therefore, self-knowledge is the most important competency for educators to impart in modern society.

Making a Difference for Students

To institutions of higher education, student success can mean elevated rates of retention, graduation, and alumni support. To parents and students, it can mean excellent grades, credentials, and jobs. Many perspectives on student success include civic involvement and societal contribution, and even extend into personal growth. But all of these student success goals derive from student well-being and self-knowledge.

We hope that this book, with its research-based, evidence based methods, will be used by higher education practitioners who want to make an even bigger difference in the lives of students in their care. Students need and want our expert guidance to help them on life's journeys to discover who they are, which direction to take, and how to manifest their highest hopes and dreams for an extraordinary quality of life.

With this book, we hope to impact

- Individual students attending institutions of higher education. Whether at a community college, middle-sized state university, small liberal arts private college, large Research I university, online university, or other institution, students require new support systems to meet their holistic needs. Students themselves have a leading role in creating a mind-set that well-being is central to their lifelong journey, the bedrock of their learning and success, and also their responsibility.
- University leaders and frontline educators. There are five functional areas aligned with student success—academic advising, career services, counseling and psychological services (CAPS), faculty teaching, and student engagement—and they all need to enhance student-centered practices and work better together. For example, there has long been a gap between those services provided by academic affairs and those provided by student affairs departments. This gap is too often filled with battles for control, resources, and power, and educators often lose sight of serving the changing and growing needs of students.
- Our readers. We hope to appeal to your higher moral sense that creating an educational environment that fosters well-being is simply the right thing to do to take care of our students. With the rise of new psychological paradigms and approaches, we are redefining student success. When we transform students' abilities to raise their levels of consciousness to take action toward making a difference in society, we can impact our communities, tackle long-standing issues, and create a better world for all people.

Education should free up our fullest human expressions possible for love, caring, kindness, healing, and understanding, and empower our full, unique, and highest potentials for a better world—our highest visions for a flourishing life.

In this mission, we feel your partnership.

Overview

This book will take you on a journey from current challenges through emerging new concepts and transformative, high-impact practices into the future.

Beginning with Chapter 1, "Higher Education and the Decline of Well-Being," we explore some of the current realities of college-aged students' physical, emotional, and psychological well-being.

In Chapter 2, "Student Success Redefined," we introduce a new model of student success that places well-being and self-knowledge at the heart of students' pathways to success. Our new model is called *Integrated Student Success* (*iSuccess*). The "i" in the name represents a holistic "integration" of each student's self-knowledge, placing the student's unique mind-set at the center of success, and also represents the integration of the key university functional areas that support student success—academic advising, career services, personal counseling, faculty teaching, and student engagement. Throughout the book we will build upon the *iSuccess* model. In this chapter we introduce the core concept of *iSuccess*—that student success depends on well-being and self-knowledge.

Chapter 3, "Higher Education's New Mission," takes a look at the emerging steps that institutions of higher education (IHEs) are taking to develop students more holistically. While higher education has not yet fully embraced well-being as the organizing core as we do in our new *iSuccess* student success model, there is a growing awareness of the need for new approaches.

In Chapter 4, "Student Success and Professional Standards," we look to see whether well-being and self-knowledge are represented in the standards of the professional organizations that guide the dedicated people working in each of the five functional areas aligned with student success—academic advising, career services, counseling and psychological services (CAPS), faculty teaching, and student engagement. These standards are addressing some but not all of the components of the *iSuccess* student success model, and professional organizations should help develop more integration across these areas to encourage higher levels of student success.

In Chapter 5, "Student Success High-Impact Practices," we build out the *iSuccess* model by presenting our three research-based, high-impact practices that demonstrate how to impart self-knowledge competencies to students throughout the college experience. The three high-impact practices are

1. The *Integrated Self* (*iSelf*) model for understanding the multiple dimensions of self-knowledge
2. *Self Across the Curriculum* (*SAC*), a pedagogy for implementing the *Integrated Self* (*iSelf*) model
3. The *Success Predictor* (*SP*), an assessment and intervention instrument

Combined, these three high-impact practices empower students to create an extraordinary life, filled with an understanding of unique potential, life purpose, and dreams.

Chapter 6, "Student Success in Practice," dives deeper into examples of promising practices from forward-thinking higher education institutions that demonstrate strong holistic approaches or progress toward the integration of the functional areas of academic advising, CAPS, faculty teaching, and student engagement. We map these promising practices to the *iSuccess* model and also provide examples of our own high-impact practices. It is our sincere hope that the reader will find these examples and discussion useful as a handbook of how to implement the *iSuccess* model.

We conclude with a short afterword containing our final thoughts and a list of resources for your continued research. There is so much more to explore in the field of education dedicated to the nourishment and well-being of students' deepest selves, the encouragement of which creates a ripple effect out into our society and future, for generations to come.

Acknowledgments

We give loving and heartfelt thanks to the many people who have shared with us their commitment to developing the whole person through education—our family, friends, colleagues, and teachers.

We also greatly appreciate all of the professional organizations mentioned in this book for granting permission to share their standards and competencies.

Special thanks go to Dr. David P. Baker, Dr. Frederick Brown, Leah Hoholick, and Rachel Paul.

Finally, we sincerely thank the dedicated student success professionals who shared examples of their excellence in action:

Dr. Rene Couture
Dr. Thomas Grites
Dr. Cynthia Love
Dr. Larry Marks
Dr. Matthew Shupp
Dr. John Wade
Dr. Jonathan Wilkes
Dr. Case Willoughby

CHAPTER 1

HIGHER EDUCATION AND THE DECLINE OF WELL-BEING

K-16 education is the most dominant force in the social construction of the selves of children, adolescents, and young adults, demanding that we embrace and teach new tools for thriving in the 21st century. In his book *The Schooled Society: The Educational Transformation of Global Culture* (2014), thought leader and professor David P. Baker indicates, "Formal education on such a vast scale in the world and in the United States culture does more than socializing children; it constructs and transforms society."

If K-16 education constructs and transforms society, then the quality of the society in which we live is largely a result of the education system. If we as college educators and professionals are doing our jobs, then why are well-being statistics among college students and people in our society so alarming?

We should be transforming people's abilities to live a good quality of life filled with personal health and wellness, as well as professional accomplishment and success. As David Baker points out in his seminal work, the proportion of children and youth attending school and how long they attend lines up nicely with gains in IQ scores. If this is true, then why haven't our abilities to increase our well-being also risen? In point of fact, the emphasis on academics over that of how to be well, and further, the overemphasis on the quantification of these skills, has contributed to the dire state of well-being in our society.

Harvard psychologist Dr. Shawn Achor's research demonstrates that only 25 percent of our success comes from the intellect. The remaining 75 percent is divided among optimism levels and social supports, and the ability to see stress as a challenge instead of a threat. "If we change our formula for happiness and success, we can change our realities" (Anchor, 2010). Further, only 10 percent of our external circumstances predict our future success, which means that 90 percent stems from the lens through which we see the world and create our realities, from the inside out.

We are encouraged by these research findings because they support the heart of our research and work on developing self-knowledge and well-being through education. We have developed methods that empower students to create a lens, which we call the self, that allows them to reenvision the formula for their success to include attributes such as happiness, optimism, and building their own meaningful networks of support.

Do higher education institutions have the responsibility to impact students' well-being? Do students want and need their higher education institutions to help them?

San Diego State University professor Dr. Jean Twenge (2009; 2010) found that five times as many high school and college students are dealing with "anxiety" and other mental health issues as youth studied in the Great Depression era. To derive these data, Twenge analyzed the responses of more than 77,000 college students who took the Minnesota Multiphasic Personality Inventory from 1938 through 2007 (Twenge et al., 2010). These findings add further evidence to support the theory that modern life is too stressful, too complex, and changing too fast for the minds that are being trained through our education system to meet the myriad of 21st-century challenges.

Further, young people are suffering in silence nationally about their despair that life can be positive, as indicated by a 2014 American Freshman Survey: "The emotional health of incoming college freshmen is at its lowest point in at least three decades." The American Freshman Survey—an annual report that is now entering its 50th year—collected responses from 153,000 full-time, first-year students at 227 four-year public and private institutions.

What has happened over the past three decades to bring us to this crisis? We have had three decades of education with emphasis on quantitative and extrinsic measures of success. Additionally, emotional and psychological well-being measures and outcomes have not been on the radar screens of our education leaders and policy makers, and parents have been led to believe that if children do well in school academically, then they will also be happy, healthy, and flourish as individuals. In other words, parents, teachers, and students have bought into the myth that testing and academic measures, and rising IQs, are the keys to future success.

The college freshman level of despair in this survey is an important metric because those adolescents just went through the K-12 public school education system, and these are the results, sadly. This demonstrates that high school college and career readiness standards need to include well-being standards and the measurement of well-being outcomes. Students need assistance when they arrive on our college campuses, and frontline college educators need to be prepared to help using new high-impact practices.

School-aged adolescents with psychological well-being have a lower risk of mental health disorders and physical health diagnoses such as anxiety, depression, obesity, cutting, substance abuse, and bullying, among others. As such, well-being is an important protective factor to impart in an adolescent's life in preparation for college and careers. Yet our system of education does not really consider well-being to be even a small part of its work. Students are primarily left to their own devices when it comes to emotional, psychological, and physical well-being.

Students and Dissonance

It is no wonder that college students have difficulty making the transition from adolescence to young adulthood. The adults in their lives who have mentored them still believe that our education system, with its misplaced emphasis on academic achievement and extrinsic measures of success, will create the conditions for a positive life-course trajectory. College students see that their parents and teachers espouse this belief, yet they hear their parents complaining about their careers, money, relationships, getting more and more abusive in the way they express themselves toward each other and them. They do not have the words or understanding to express that this is not quite right—but they feel it at the core of their being. This is not to say that career and material pursuits do not have value. We are all for grit, persistence, and accomplishment, but only if they are intrinsically motivated and do not come at the cost of well-being.

Students have difficulty trusting themselves because they do not have a way of viewing the world, their realities, and what is important because the world is telling them one thing and they are experiencing another. This inability keeps them off kilter, not quite feeling that they are on a solid foundation to know and understand what they are seeing (i.e., circumstances) and experiencing (i.e., beliefs)—outside influences and values that they feel are wrong.

Today's college students believe that by following the rules of the education system, they will have a great life. And yet the trajectory of their quality of life is less than that of their parents. They are more apt to see their parents struggle day to day with increased stressors of simply meeting their financial obligations. They are witness to the increased use and abuse of drugs and alcohol in the attempt to self-medicate to obtain happiness and fulfill the image that the complexities of life are handled. They see abusive behavior and language used by political leaders in our society to either demean others or to obstruct the political process and governing, and in their own homes. They see that leaders allowed the perpetrators of the greatest recession since the Great Depression to go unpunished for wrongdoing, and in fact be rewarded. They see a chasm between what they know to be true for them, their inner compass of good, and the external realities they bump up against every day.

They often will have to move back into their parents' home because they cannot find a good paying job to live on their own and chart their own path and life. They are burdened with loan debt that may take a lifetime to pay off, and this weight feels like a big obstacle, obstructing the path to a life filled with possibilities, which is beyond their current realities. They are made to feel that they do not measure up, that somehow they are not good enough to compete and make it in our democracy and capitalistic society, where the top 1 percent seemingly have all the advantages. To adolescents and young adults, this is true; this is a part of their realities.

College-aged students see well-being and success through the omnipresence of cultural beliefs that appear to put the individual first but really only value selected individuals. The celebrity culture works hard at making it known that special people are living the dream. In our 24/7 society, we see Facebook, Instagram, and other social media act as evidence that everyone everywhere appear to be living the good life. Therefore, the still-developing adolescents that arrive at our campus door every new school year have an embedded belief that college is the pathway to the good life that they have absorbed for the previous eighteen years. It is now a part of their way of being and psychic DNA.

As they go through their college experiences, which reflect these cultural beliefs, they begin to put it together that their beliefs and visions for the good life, along with college itself, may not provide the pathway to true success. They know something is off, that something is not quite right, that they do not have the answer, methods, or paradigm of thinking that will empower their success in life. Often, resignation (or at least sadness and doubt) takes over and replaces the hopes and dreams they once had upon arrival. This is when students dropout, either emotionally or literally from their programs, when they no longer can see how college can help them realize their dreams, or at least help them understand those dreams. It is our job to teach those methods and paradigms that empower a life course that fulfills greater understanding, a greater consciousness, of the good life.

When children, adolescents, and young adults are told one thing yet experience another, this creates a cognitive dissonance (Festinger, 1957), leading to stress and anxiety. This is the feeling of uncomfortable tension that comes from holding two conflicting thoughts in the mind at the same time. Dissonance increases with

- The importance of the subject to us
- How strongly the dissonant thoughts conflict
- Our inability to rationalize and explain away the conflict

Dissonance is often strongest when we believe something about ourselves and then do or experience something against that belief. For example, we are good and talented, yet not able to fully feel the joy and satisfaction that come from accomplishing and getting good grades in school. Therefore, what happens is that young people remove the importance of a belief or set of beliefs that they feel contribute to the dissonance, such as fully investing oneself into a task or situation. They take themselves away from the current reality or situation and attempt to find another reality that works better for them. People who experience trauma (e.g., posttraumatic stress disorder) to varying degrees dissociate themselves from life. They have learned to reduce the emotional pain by not feeling so deeply about a particular situation, life in general, or sadly, themselves.

We all know the person who chooses a self-destructive lifestyle, that person who once got or gets perfect grades, starred or stars on the athletic field, and who was or is a perfect child at home, then turns to drugs, alcohol, aggressive behavior, cutting, or suicide. Once this person starts harming themselves or others, then a Diagnostic Statistical Manual (DSM) diagnosis can be made if this person seeks help. But brewing before self-destructive behaviors manifest is usually a lack of a feeling of self-esteem or self-knowledge. Most directly, those who actually engage in self-harm or harm to others are not aware of their unique life purpose or dreams for their life and do not know how to access either. Therefore they blame others or themselves for their feeling of being stuck in a state of not being able to feel, with a condition of dissociation. So too is the student who seems to be laid back, not motivated by anything in particular, just going through the motions of, as one example, enrolling into classes and getting by academically. They do not use all of their innate talents, skills, and abilities to see and achieve their unique potentials. They seem to be drifting through life, lost about which direction to take, and are influenced by the next big thing or group think.

Students do not have to do harm to be self-destructive. The absence of a growth mind-set—one where they actively seek ways to develop emotionally, psychologically, and physically toward their unique potentials—will not necessarily be in the DSM handbook, but this is equally harmful to them and their futures.

Student Concerns

According to the National Survey of College Counseling Centers (2014), the top ten primary presenting concerns of students, listed in descending order, are

1. Anxiety
2. Depression
3. Relationship problems
4. Stress
5. Academic performance
6. Family
7. Interpersonal functioning
8. Grief or loss
9. Mood instability
10. Adjustment to a new environment

Often these concerns, left unaddressed, represent risk factors for additional harmful behaviors such as suicide and self-harm such as cutting, drug and alcohol abuse, sexual assault, and aggressive interpersonal relationships, among others.

College Students Are Not Well

According to the National Survey of College Counseling Centers (2014), 94 percent of counseling and psychological services (CAPS) professionals report that "recent trends toward greater numbers of students with some psychological problems continue to be true on their campuses."

Campus statistics are alarming and have reached a critical stage:

- 24 percent of students harm themselves through cutting or other forms of self-mutilation.
- 23 percent of women are sexually assaulted on campus.
- 5 times as many high school and college students are dealing with anxiety and other mental health issues as youth of the same age who were studied in the Great Depression era.

- A survey of college counseling centers has found that more than half their clients have severe psychological problems, an increase of 13 percent in just two years.
- Anxiety and depression are the most common mental health diagnoses among college students, according to the Center for Collegiate Mental Health (2016).
- Currently, roughly 1,100 college students take their lives each year.
- 71 percent of students at one private Ivy League university get blackout drunk, with 28 percent doing so at least once or twice a week.
- Over 40 percent of students at one Big Ten University do not feel safe, according to a 2015 sexual aggression study.
- CAPS directors report that 52 percent of counseling center clients have severe psychological problems (up from 44 percent in 2013).
- 44 percent of college students experience periods of severe distress (depression, anxiety, panic attacks, suicidal ideation, etc.)

Well-Being in the United States

According to some experts, hopelessness, despair, and disappointment about economic and social well-being are the leading causes of an overall decline in our nation's well-being. What this means is that adults in our society do not have a set of tools to draw upon when life gets difficult. They do not have the mental framework that provides a way for them to overcome childhood trauma or sadness about unrealized expectations in early or mid-adulthood. This presents an opportunity for higher education institutions to supplement what is missing in our society, to impact troubling statistics such as the following, taken from the National Survey of College Counseling Centers (2014), National Alliance on Mental Health (2015), and the National Center for Health Statistics (Curtis et al., 2016):

- The burden of mental illness in the United States is among the highest of all diseases, and mental health disorders are among the most common causes of disability. The most recent national data shows that in 2014, an estimated 43.6 million (18.1 percent) adults aged 18 years and over had experienced some form of mental illness, and an estimated 9.8 million (4.2 percent) adults had a serious mental illness.
- Suicide rates have increased 24 percent in the past 15 years in the United States, with the highest rate increases among women.

- Suicide among adolescents and young adults is increasing and among the leading causes of death.
- Over 2/3 of Americans are overweight or obese.
- The United States uses 80 percent of the world's opiates (prescription drugs), while having only 5 percent of the world's population.

Long before They Arrive on Campus

Approximately 20 percent of children experience depression before they reach adulthood, with another 29 percent of adolescents in grades 9–12 reporting feeling sad or hopeless almost every day for an extended period such that it interferes with their ability to do school work or even attend school. To underscore the point that mental health needs are not being met prior to attending college, the US Centers for Disease Control and Prevention (CDC) reported that ten- to fourteen-year-old girls had the highest growth of suicides between 1999 and 2014. Just think about how emotionally troubling life must be for these young girls, and just how oblivious parents, educators, and health care professionals are to observing and diagnosing the symptoms. Even worse, no one has called for new prevention methods to stem the tide.

The rising incidences of anxiety, depression, and suicide in college students start long before they arrive on our campuses. Yet they consider our ability to help them address their mental health and well-being one indicator of a good college experience, worthy of the investment.

Almost all teens experience at least one or more of these factors in their adolescent years (between eleven and twenty-four years of age):

- Abuse and neglect
- Chronic illness or other physical conditions
- Family history of depression or mental illness (Between 20 percent and 50 percent of teens suffering from depression have a family member with depression or some other mental disorder.)
- Untreated mental or substance-abuse problems (Approximately two-thirds of teens with major depression also battle another mood disorder such as dysthymia, anxiety, antisocial behaviors, or substance abuse.)
- Trauma or disruptions at home, including divorce or deaths of parents
- Low self-esteem or confidence
- External locus of control orientation (versus internal)
- Lack of meaning and direction in life through unformed life purpose and/or dreams

Risk factors for depression and suicide among teens vary; for example, teen girls develop depression twice as often as boys. However, of the challenges listed above, most can be ameliorated by teaching adolescents a mental model or mind-set that helps them understand who they are and what they might be going through.

Anxiety and Loneliness

According to the American College Health Association's 2015 survey, 54 percent of students reported "feeling overwhelming anxiety." Students have not been taught how to manage the growing complexities of life away from home, competition for academic accomplishments and hence good jobs, and social engagement with peers and mentors. They simply do not know how to make this major human development transition. Anxiety is an emotion, a feeling that results from not having a mental framework that allows for changes to one's mind-set and therefore emotional regulation. As with other well-being challenges discussed previously, anxiety can lead to dissociation, the inability to feel emotions, and is an antecedent to more acute mental health issues. This is a major reason why we should and could be doing more to prevent it in over one half of our students.

Students who think that their academic courses are competitive increase their odds of positively screening for depression by 40 percent and anxiety by 70 percent. Students have bought into the belief system so prevalent in our society that grades are the key to success in their careers and life that they literally make themselves mentally ill. They do not have another model or paradigm of life or set of tools to figure out who they are and what is important to them. No one is teaching them how to create a paradigm of self that enhances their well-being as they go through life's challenges—whether in school, with romantic relationships, or career choices.

They are left to flounder directionless in a fast-paced modern society that leaves them feeling more and more isolated and lonely. Psychologist Carl Jung (1875–1961) said, "Loneliness does not come from having no people around you, but from being unable to communicate the things that seem important to you, or from holding certain views which others find inadmissible" (Jung, 1961). This quote captures the essence of loneliness and one reason that explains the above tragic list of well-being statistics.

When a student does not know who he is, at a conscious or knowing level, he cannot talk about what is going on inside of himself—his inner thoughts and feelings. This leads him to perceive himself as different, weird, or abnormal, without the resources or skills to discuss these feelings and therefore develop meaningful relationships. This results in a wide range of emotions, from anger and rage to sadness, and behaviors such as self-harm and abuse of others.

Sexual Violence on Campus

With President Obama's requirements established by the Violence Against Women Reauthorization Act (VAWA) signed into law March 7, 2013, we are compelled to highlight the importance of addressing violence against women on college campuses as a part of the whole picture on well-being.

According to the 2015 Association of American Universities (AAU) Campus Survey, "For college women seniors, the number reporting nonconsensual sexual contact of any kind carried out by force or while incapacitated was even higher than the 23% for all female college students: 26% of female seniors said they had experienced it at some point during their four years in college. At some of the country's most elite schools, that number climbed even higher: 34% for University of Michigan female seniors, 32% at Yale and 29% at Harvard."

The results of the Sexual Misconduct Climate Survey conducted by The Pennsylvania State University and released in April 2016 include these troubling statistics that underscore the heightened need to address aggressive behaviors sooner versus later: among undergraduates, 27.5 percent of women; 6.2 percent of men; and 25.7 percent of lesbian, gay, bisexual, transgendered, and queer respondents said they had been the victim of at least one instance of sexual assault or attempt.

In this report, Penn State concluded, "It is not easy to define the scope of the problem, either nationally or at Penn State. The Centers for Disease Control estimates that one in five women in the United States will be raped in her lifetime, and 63% of American women have experienced some form of sexual violence."

"The data on abusive drinking among students at Penn State, and at nearly every other college or university, can be staggering" (Penn State Task Force, 2015). Higher education leaders are struggling to understand why students behave with such aggression and to define the antecedents.

However, we do not accept, nor does the research support, the conclusion drawn in this Penn State task force report: "It has never been fashionable to speak openly about the relationship between sexual abuse and substance abuse. The linkage quickly invites 'victim blaming.' But the Pennsylvania Coalition Against Rape (PCAR) reports that at least 80% of college students who were sexually assaulted were under the influence of alcohol, and the percentage of assailants who were misusing alcohol is likely greater still. Even victim advocates within the Penn State community quickly acknowledge that the two issues are profoundly interconnected." The real root cause of the problem is not alcohol, but rather the emptiness within the abusers, and through our research and work, we know we can lead, educate, and create psychologically healthy people.

While we empathize with educators facing these overwhelming challenges and have listened patiently to this university and other universities saying they are without effective methods to prevent either abusive drinking or abusive behaviors, it is beyond our comprehension—given our expertise and the emergence of promising state-of-the-art methods to support and promote positive mental health and well-being—that our colleges and universities approach these issues and problems with a mind-set of helplessness.

We do not intend to communicate that this issue is uniquely a Penn State problem; all higher education institutions are required to face the new challenges presented by our nation's mental health epidemic. Certainly, all university leaders are searching for a new model and methods of how to help students. At the Penn State Board of Trustees meeting in May 2016, the Vice President of Student Affairs asserted that we just do not know what to do about these problems, and "I don't think we will resolve that question with one answer" (Falce, 2016). This expresses the complexity of the problems and the lack of an effective framework or model to resolve these. At Penn State, "nonsuicidal self-injury, like cutting, is up 16 percent. Suicidal ideation has about doubled," and yet CAPS espouses its extensive research about student mental health as taking action to address it. It follows that the problems are more acute, and that somehow the process of collecting the statistics will resolve the issues, with CAPS going so far as to assert in an article that the well-being issues on campus have not reached crisis levels (Locke, 2016). We would suggest telling that to those students who ideate suicide or cut themselves.

Our point is that higher education institutions are not taking the kinds of *preventative* measures that can help students on their campuses become better people. We suggest that our new student success model would go a long way to reduce incidences of destructive behavior and, moreover, help focus attention on the heart of the problem that leads to excess drinking and then violent behavior. We can all agree that when so many students have been victimized, something needs to be done, *preventatively*.

Depression

Symptoms of depression in adolescents and young adults include

- Sadness or hopelessness
- Irritability, anger, or hostility
- Tearfulness or frequent crying
- Withdrawal from friends and family
- Loss of interest or enjoyment in activities
- Changing in eating and sleeping habits
- Feelings of worthlessness and guilt
- Lack of enthusiasm and motivation
- Fatigue or lack of energy
- Difficulty concentrating and making decisions
- Thoughts of death or suicide

We need to create early intervention or prevention programs that teach strategies for how to think about the world, manage one's thoughts, body, emotions, and overall well-being. In the absence of these programs, multiple disorders will most likely materialize in a student's life during college years. If we allow students to internalize these symptoms during their learning careers, then these will continue into adulthood and be a recurring lifelong problem. We have an opportunity to help students understand risk and protective factors for a successful life.

Suicide

We find it alarming that the Substance Abuse and Mental Health Services Administration (SAMSHA) Suicide Prevention Resource Center's (SPRC's) list for suicide prevention does not consider self-knowledge an important "protective factor," where we have found it is the number one protective factor (Brzycki, 2013).

To demonstrate our point, here are the key points about risk and protective factors for suicide prevention, according to the SPRC (2014, used with permission):

- Risk and protective factors play a critical role in the prevention of suicide for both individuals and communities.
- Risk factors are not warning signs.

- Major risk factors include prior suicide attempt(s), mood disorders, substance abuse, and access to lethal means.
- Major protective factors include effective mental health care, connectedness, problem-solving skills, and contacts with caregivers.
- Risk and protective factors provide targets for intervention in both individuals and communities: decreasing risk factors generally decreases risk, and increasing protective factors generally decreases risk.
- Risk and protective factors vary between individuals and across settings.
- Suicide prevention efforts should begin with a strategic planning process that, among other goals, identifies and targets specific risk and protective factors for intervention.

The SPRC suggests "problem-solving skills" and "connectedness" as protective factors, but there are far more components to self-knowledge than these. The SPRC is failing to provide a comprehensive prevention and intervention approach.

Self-knowledge is not fully considered by leading health care organizations such as the SAMSHA and SPRC, among others, because of the adherence to the medical model of illness and treatment still predominant in our society today. Healthcare is still focused on treatment rather than the many dimensions of prevention. Higher education counseling and psychological services follows this same health care paradigm, in spite of numerous research studies that demonstrate the causal relationship between mental and behavioral health outcomes. Further, higher education CAPS follow SAMSHA guidelines. Therefore, it is no wonder that the senior student affairs administrator at a Research I university stood before his Board of Trustees and basically threw up his hands and said, "We do not know what to do!"

Physical Health

Research has shown that psychological stress can contribute to increased rates of heart disease, decreased immune system functioning, and premature aging. Other research has demonstrated that cognitions, attitudes, beliefs, values, social support, prayer, and meditation can reduce psychological stress and contribute to positive health outcomes. Consequently, over the past decade, the National Institutes of Health (NIH) has increased its efforts to encourage and support health and behavior research, of which mind-body research is one component.

Over the previous fifteen years, numerous mind-body centers and research programs have been funded by the NIH Office of Behavioral and Social Sciences Research (OBSSR). Here are some examples:

- Columbia University: Mind-Body-Behavioral Medicine Clinical Trials Infrastructure
- Johns Hopkins University: Center for Mind-Body Research
- New York University School of Medicine: Development of a Mind-Body Center at NYUSOM
- Ohio State University: Center for Stress and Wound Healing
- Rutgers University: The State University of New Jersey Center for the Study of Health Beliefs and Behavior
- University of California–Berkeley: Social Disparities in the Early Neurobiology of Stress
- University of California–Los Angeles: Mind/Brain/Body Interactions in Stress-Related Disorders
- University of Miami: Center for Psycho-Oncology Research
- University of Michigan: Michigan Interdisciplinary Center on Social Inequality, Mind, and Body
- University of North Carolina–Chapel Hill: Gastrointestinal Biopsychosocial Research Center
- University of Pittsburgh Medical Center/Carnegie Mellon University: Understanding Shared Psychobiological Pathways
- University of Pittsburgh/Carnegie Mellon University: Pittsburgh Mind-Body Center II
- University of Rochester: Rochester Center for Mind-Body Research
- University of Texas: Medical Branch of Psychoneuroimmunology, Stress, and Healthy Aging in Hispanics
- University of Utah: Utah Center for Exploring Mind-Body Interactions
- University of Wisconsin: Mechanisms of Mind-Body Interaction: Emotional Interface

The results of these studies have been robust and conclusively reinforced the mind-body connection. If the NIH has funded these studies to explore the mental and behavioral causes of well-being, then why have educators largely ignored these? One plausible explanation is that awareness of the mind-body connection and the study of human emotions do not fit their existing paradigms.

Demands of a Complex World

Long before the proliferation of social media and the increased pace of life due to the influx of technology in our lives, more than two decades ago, Harvard University Professor Robert Kegan asserted that we do not have the mental paradigm or way of thinking to be able to handle modern life with its inherent complexities and stressors: "The expectations upon us . . . demand something more than mere behavior, the acquisition of specific skills, or the mastery of particular knowledge. They make demands on our minds, on how we know, on the complexity of our consciousness" (Kegan, 1994, p. 5). We cannot escape the powerful influence of culture in modern society when shaping personal meaning. We need a new mind-set, a way of structuring our world, to be effective human beings in the 21st century, and higher education is where this new mind-set can be taught and developed.

Students' Changing Needs

College-aged young adults are struggling to develop their own pathways for a positive life-course trajectory, purposefully, with meaningful direction. This next generation of students, labeled Generation Z or GenZ, want to be thoroughly engaged in their education and lives. They value education if it is hands-on or leads to their ability to make a difference in the world. Additionally, they value education if it prepares them for a better quality of life than that of their parents, not only financially but in terms of wellness through a better understanding of who they are. In one conversation with a college junior, he stated, "My academic advisor only cares about my number of credits and if I am taking the right courses," expressing the desire to get more in-depth guidance from an important person in his life to help him develop keys to success not only academically but also for his career and life.

Consider that Malala Yousafzai, the Pakistani activist for female education and the youngest-ever Nobel Prize laureate, is a GenZ member and is representative of using education to make a real-world impact. She is an excellent role model for her fellow GenZers.

In a recent study by the Lumina Foundation (2015), it was found that the makeup of the higher education student population has changed, and it is no longer made up of primarily eighteen to twenty-two year olds.

- 38 percent of undergraduates are older than twenty-five and therefore often balance work, families, and school.
- 58 percent work while in school.

- 26 percent of students are raising children.
- Only 13 percent live on campus.
- 40 percent attend part time.
- Enrollment among Hispanic students tripled over the last fifteen years.
- Black student enrollment grew by 72 percent.

Lumina concluded that many "students are struggling to navigate the outdated higher education system." Today's students need new approaches to understand how to be successful in their learning careers and beyond, and in particular, how to manage the complex set of stressors in their lives that could at any moment derail their path to a positive life course. According to Lumina, "Between financial strains, work responsibilities and childcare, today's students have much more on their minds than just school, and many lack the social and emotional support they need to persist."

We have researched the holistic needs of changing student populations and developed high-impact practices and student success models that meet these needs through a combination of internal and external protective factors:

- Self-understanding
- Awareness of pathways for achieving one's potential for success in school, career, and life
- A sense of empowerment to control one's own destiny in life
- Increased presence of a respected mentor
- Deep and meaningful relationships with mentor(s)
- Socioemotional supports
- More real-world learning (RWL) opportunities (These are opportunities that connect academic learning to community projects or working at a job.)
- Professional training, leading toward a successful career

Completion Rates

The most common metrics used by colleges and universities to measure "student success" involve retention—dropout versus completion rates. While these completion rates do matter, they are primarily institution focused, and students drop out if the obstacles that they face are not addressed while attending college.

We believe dropout rates point to students' lack of purposeful direction. Nationwide, only approximately 45 percent of college students earned a bachelor's degree within six years (US Department of Education, National Center for Education Statistics, 2009).

At Clarion University, a Pennsylvania State System of Higher Education (PASSHE) institution where coauthor Henry taught, only 53 percent of students finished within six years(just a bit better than the national average), and only 24 percent of students in Clarion's College of Education and Human Services completed their programs of study.

We need to be more aware of the implications of these alarming statistics when you consider that by 2020, over 69 percent of jobs will require a college education. So we concede that retention is important, not so much as an institutional metric, upon which others may focus, but rather as an indicator of students' abilities to overcome immense obstacles.

Students drop out due to a wide array of reasons. Increased stressors that reduce satisfaction and serve as obstacles to degree completion are

- Rising tuition and living costs associated with earning credentials
- Reduced college readiness of new student pools
- Increased number of critical life transitions (readiness to develop from childhood to adolescence and from adolescence to young adulthood, having to work to help supplement family financial support, working full time to support a family, among others)
- Limited internships, real-world projects, or leadership opportunities to build professional competencies prior to graduation
- Reduced job opportunities that allow for a good standard of living
- Young adults' growing awareness of these reduced career opportunities and deepening resignation that life can be great

According to a 2015 study by the National Center for Education Statistics, six-year graduation rates for first-time, full-time students who began seeking a bachelor's degree in fall 2007 varied according to institutional level of selectivity. In particular, graduation rates were highest at postsecondary degree-granting institutions that were the most selective (i.e., had the lowest admissions acceptance rates), and graduation rates were lowest at institutions that were the least selective (i.e., had open admissions policies). For example, at four-year institutions with open admissions policies, 34 percent of students completed a bachelor's degree within six years. At four-year institutions where the acceptance rate was less than 25 percent of applicants, the six-year graduation rate was 89 percent.

We suspect that the differences in rates stem from the more selective institutions offering better student support services, while the usual interpretation would be that students from less selective IHEs bring more risk factors (US Department of Education, National Center for Education Statistics, 2015).

Retention itself should not be our focus, but rather student well-being, student satisfaction, and student-directed success pathways. The lack of self-knowledge is a risk factor leading to risky behaviors, lack of motivation, and detachment from academic studies, and decreased resilience required to overcome obstacles. Dropout rates from colleges point to students' lack of self-understanding and purposeful direction.

We need to focus our attention on the inner selves of adolescents and young adults attending higher education, not those variables that are too often used to explain poor retention and completion rates. Too much attention is paid to external circumstances such as income levels, as in "the odds of finishing are tied closely to income. Children from families who earn more than $90, 000 have a one-in-two chance of getting a bachelor's degree by age 24. That falls to a one-in-17 chance for those earning under $35, 000" (Selingo, *Student Success*, 2015, p. 8). Now that we have increased access to higher education for underserved populations, policy makers are requiring higher education institutions to invest even more into support services and programs that ensure student success.

But now we have a dilemma. It is too expensive to focus upon requiring institutions to offer more and more services simply to meet retention and completion metrics. According to a recent survey, "positions in student services now make up nearly a third of professional jobs on campuses, more than three times the number of administrative positions" (Selingo, *Student Success*, 2015, p. 10). Our colleges and universities may simply be throwing money at hiring "student success" professionals, and this most likely cannot be sustained. However, to implement a comprehensive model of student success and best practices that empowers students to take charge of their own definition of success, we need to give students the tools to chart their own pathways using the extensive resources that are made available to them by American colleges and universities. If and when we do this, student affairs and academic affairs will be more effective when impacting students.

Internal versus External Selves

> The individual has within himself vast resources for self-understanding, for altering his self-concept, his attitudes, and his self-directed behavior—and that these resources can be tapped if only a definable climate of facilitative psychological attitudes can be provided.
>
> —Rogers, 1986, p. 135

We can conclude from the preceding summary of well-being statistics and challenges that children and adolescents are not taught by families, parents, or educators how to cope in modern life. Children and adolescents are being taught how to do well on standardized tests. They are taught to put on an external face that everything is fine. Further, and most often, adolescents do not know enough about who they are to know if their well-being is where it should be and even what well-being is. They are not taught that it is perfectly all right to ask for help in order to address academic challenges or relationship dynamics or gain self-understanding in a world where we are well-versed in making it look like we are succeeding in all domains of life—the next selfie and Facebook post will demonstrate this to our friends and the world. As an antidote, we advocate for higher education institutions to create a "definable climate of facilitative psychological attitudes" that will allow students to tap into their "vast resources."

Today's youth find themselves focused on external goals such as wealth, fame, and success; attainment of school-based measures; and college selection and loans, to name a few, all the while struggling with unhealthy levels of emotional dependence on technology. Rarely do they learn to navigate internal goals, such as feelings, self-understanding, relationship intimacy, and purpose and dreams in life, among others. It is no wonder that young people are experiencing that it all feels beyond their control to live a high quality of life, a flourishing life to the level of their unique potentials and what they can envision.

Primary driving motivations for all human beings are to see and achieve full and unique potentials in life, to matter, to make an impact, to live a good life. Therefore, from numerous points of view—economic, sociological, psychological, and educational—it is important to ask the following questions: Why don't people achieve their full potentials in life? What pathways to potential are available to us as human beings?

Higher education scholars and practitioners from academic advising, career and personal counseling, faculty teaching, and student engagement consider the idea of potential and student development from their particular points of view and functional measures of success, not from their students' individual psychological and physical well-being. Even from the disciplines of psychology and medicine, external risk and protective factors are considered most often, before the inner self, which might not even be considered at all.

Looking through the self-knowledge lens, therefore, emotional, psychological, and physical well-being, or wellness, are functions of learning about the self. But where in our society does this learning occur? And where should it occur? Higher education student success processes are potentially the most direct applications for learning about the self and are at the heart of our new student success model and high-impact practices.

An important distinction is that of the "internal" or "inner" self, or what occurs within the mind of the person, and "external" or "outside" self, or what circumstances occur outside the mind of the person but within his or her realm of experience. This is important in that the majority of studies conducted in numerous fields that teachers, advisors, and counselors draw upon for validation of new concepts address the external or circumstantial variables of the self. A good example is that of attributing academic success to socioeconomic levels—that students who come from less advantaged home lives will most likely not do as well in their academic studies as students from privileged backgrounds. In our experience of working with individuals from all walks of life, it is their inner constitution, character, mind-set, intrinsic motivations, and dreams for a good life that make the difference, not their external circumstances.

Who among us has gone through life without knowing who we are, or without having a paradigm to guide us in understanding who we are and why we do the things we do? Perhaps if we had known who we were, we could have accessed deeper experiences in our relationships, or been better able to handle emotional upset in the workplace, as two examples. Perhaps we could heal those adverse childhood experiences with greater emotional intelligence. Perhaps we could have had more accomplishments academically, with better job prospects that more closely mirrored our innate nature and talents. By gaining a more thorough understanding of our unique potential, we can find a more direct pathway to reaching it as we navigate this fast-paced, rapidly changing modern life. During the times in which overwhelming personal and professional crises threaten our mental and physical health, we must find the psychological and emotional tools we need to get through these periods.

How many of us either have lived or now live a life of quiet desperation, hoping to one day be able to manifest our unique and full potentials in life?

This is the major underlying antecedent to drug and alcohol abuse, abusive behaviors, self-harm, and a sense of resignation that our potential will never be manifest. Who among us has ever given up on the importance of dreaming, or envisioning a better world and life?

From the external circumstantial view, we discuss how colleges and universities need to change by saying that our higher education institutions need to do more to impact student wellness holistically. From the internal, inner-self and human-centric view, we sense the need for changes in higher education because we feel that the potential of people is not being manifest. We see that we are not taking care of the highest species on this planet, human beings, so how can we ever expect to take care of the rest of the planet? We keep doing more of the same thing, expecting a different result.

When we do not have the inner resources to meet external demands, we blame others, act out in aggression to those most vulnerable, or withdraw. This is important to recognize when attempting to understand the inner-external dynamic and achieve a healthy balance between them.

It is our intent to provide a set of high-impact practices to address such acute needs—student well-being needs.

Final Thoughts

Our own research indicates that for too many young people and college-aged students, quality of life is not good and getting worse, and students are filled with psychological and physical unease that manifests itself in numerous health-related illnesses. The CDC found those states with high depression rates also have higher than average rates of obesity, heart disease, diabetes, and other illnesses. Bottom line, students are entering colleges and universities with expanded needs and more mental and physical challenges and illnesses. And these well-being needs have not been adequately measured, let alone addressed, by faculty, frontline advisors, or university leaders.

Just ask any counseling and psychological services professional in your college or university and they will tell you that your students are not well emotionally, psychologically, and physically; those most responsible for their well-being—advisers and faculty members—have not been provided with a way to analyze and help solve the problem.

Institutional leaders, frontline advisers, and faculty members have been led to believe that if college students do well academically, then they will also be happy, healthy, and flourishing in higher education and life. That is a false belief that we should not perpetuate. Even if students take full advantage of internships, engagement activities, and research projects with faculty members, these experiences may not help them flourish if they do not help develop the whole person.

Evidence abounds that following the rules of our society to excel in schooling and the K-16 education system does not necessarily translate into a good quality of life, a life filled with happiness, health, and flourishing.

CHAPTER 2

STUDENT SUCCESS REDEFINED

The need is clear for a new student success model that places well-being at the center of students' college experience and moreover empowers students to define success for themselves.

Student success is simply not possible without well-being. Think about it: Can we say a student is succeeding if he or she is not well? Can students say that they are succeeding if they are filled with anxiety day to day and have difficulty functioning? The answer to these questions is self-evident. Therefore, we can assert that student success demands wellness.

Student Success Requires Well-Being

Student success requires well-being; therefore we need to understand what well-being is. A holistic model implies a multidimensional understanding of component parts that make up "wellness," as depicted in Figure 1. We use wellness and well-being interchangeably.

Wellness or well-being is not simply the absence of mental or physical illness. Rather, it is the more positive connotation of how well your life is going. Well-being encompasses emotional health, vitality, and satisfaction; life direction; ability to make a difference; the quality of one's relationships; and living a good life (Brown and LaJambe, 2016). We also want to make it clear that people with physical ailments or obstacles, whether congenital, acute, or chronic, can have well-being if they take care of themselves and balance the other dimensions of wellness.

We cannot think of wellness or well-being in one single dimension, meaning each of the eight dimensions of wellness overlap into a whole or holistic model. One of the dimensions of wellness in Figure 1 is "occupational," or

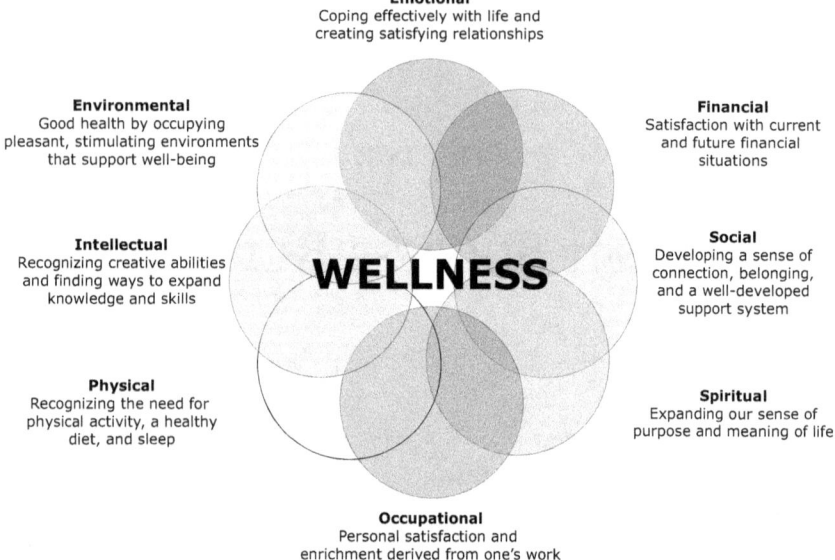

Figure 1. A Model of Wellness. *Adapted from Swarbick (2006).*

the satisfaction or sense of accomplishment from a career. This dimension interacts with "intellectual, financial, social, emotional," and most likely all eight dimensions to varying degrees. In higher education currently, well-being is often reserved for the counseling professionals in the counseling and psychological services (CAPS) functional area, but wellness is actually a broader concept that includes understanding purpose and meaning in life, developing a sense of belonging, taking care of physical needs, understanding intellectual strengths and unique capabilities, understanding financial management and support for lifestyle choices, and developing the ability to feel a full range of emotions. This broader definition of well-being requires the involvement of all the college student success functions, so as to utilize each other's strengths in support of student success.

An Expanded Definition of Well-Being

According to researcher and University of Pennsylvania professor Martin Seligman, well-being is a construct within the branch of psychology known as positive psychology. Well-being comes from our personal experiences in life—meaning that we can and do experience well-being in numerous ways.

We construct our meaning of well-being made up of these component parts (Seligman 2001, p. 24):

- Positive emotion (of which happiness and life satisfaction are elements)
- Engagement (of which motivation, both intrinsic and extrinsic, are elements)
- Relationships (empowering others while empowering self)
- Meaning (life purpose and the ability to create meaning)
- Achievement (accomplishing results that indicate whether or not one's life purpose is manifest)

To further round out our understanding of well-being, positive psychologist and University of Wisconsin professor and researcher Dr. Carol Ryff (1985; 1998; 2003) has a compatible view and has developed psychological well-being scales consisting of these dimensions:

- *Autonomy.* A person who would score high is self-determining and independent, able to resist social pressures to think and act in certain ways, regulates behavior from within, and evaluates one's self by personal standards. Someone who would score low is concerned about the expectations and evaluations of others, relies on judgments of others to make important decisions, and conforms to social pressures to think and act in certain ways.
- *Environmental mastery.* A high scorer has a sense of mastery and competence in managing the environment, controls a complex array of external activities, makes effective use of surrounding opportunities, and is able to choose or create contexts suitable to personal needs and values. A low scorer has difficulty managing everyday affairs, feels unable to change or improve surrounding contexts, is unaware of surrounding opportunities, and lacks a sense of control over the external world.
- *Personal growth.* A high scorer has a feeling of continued development, sees the self as growing and expanding, is open to new experiences, has a sense of realizing his or her potential, sees improvement in self and behavior over time, and is changing in ways that reflect more self-knowledge and effectiveness. A low scorer has a sense of personal stagnation, lacks a sense of improvement or expansion over time, feels bored and uninterested with life, and feels unable to develop new attitudes or behaviors.
- *Positive relations with others.* A high scorer has warm, satisfying, trusting relationships with others; is concerned about the welfare of others;

is capable of strong empathy, affection, and intimacy; and understands the give and take of human relationships. A low scorer has few close, trusting relationships with others; finds it difficult to be warm, open, and concerned about others; is isolated and frustrated in interpersonal relationships; and is unwilling to make compromises to sustain important ties with others.

- *Purpose in life.* A high scorer has goals in life and a sense of directedness, feels there is meaning to present and past life, holds beliefs that give life purpose, and has aims and objectives for living. A low scorer lacks a sense of meaning in life, has few goals or aims, lacks a sense of direction, does not see the purpose of previous life experiences, and has no outlook or beliefs that give life meaning.
- *Self-acceptance.* A high scorer possesses a positive attitude toward the self, acknowledges and accepts multiple aspects of self including good and bad qualities, and feels positive about previous life experiences. A low scorer feels dissatisfied with self, is disappointed with what has occurred in past life, is troubled about certain personal qualities, and wishes to be different from what he or she is.

High scorers using the Ryff scale of psychological well-being have a lower risk of mental health disorders or physical health diagnoses such as obesity, cutting, and substance abuse, among others.

As such, well-being is an important protective factor to impart in college students' learning career to help foster increased quality of life.

Self-Knowledge

The most commonly used definition of *self* is the personality or character—the combination of emotions, thoughts, feelings, and so on—that make a person different from other people. But based on our research and views expressed by psychologists, sociologists, and philosophers, we have come to see the self as a dynamic context for living rather than a static entity. Additionally, the self proactively defines and shapes the world. The self changes over time and helps create one's own experiences, rather than merely being shaped by experiences.

In the past few years, talking about the self in education often devolves to only one dimension, that of self-esteem, and unfortunately, self-esteem has taken on the connotation of indulgence and selfishness. But the real definition of self-esteem is nothing of the kind. It is feeling respect for, and confidence and satisfaction in, one's abilities—leading to desirable and healthy perspectives. Further, self-esteem is only one of over thirty attributes or dimensions of the self we have researched. (We present the full model and research in Chapter 5). The self is truly multidimensional.

It is helpful to think about the concept and importance of self-knowledge on the evolutionary continuum of human psychology. Contributions to this concept include Freud's psychoanalysis, Jung's psychological types, Piaget's genetic psychology, the personality and humanistic psychology offered by Maslow and Rogers, the sociocultural model of Vygotsky, the social learning theories of Bandura, and the model of information processing and new perspectives of mind offered by Bruner and Damasio. Within the past decade, we have witnessed breakthroughs in our understanding of what it means to be human through positive psychology, introduced by Seligman, Csikszentmihalyi, Deci and Ryan, Ryff, and more. All these bodies of knowledge helped integrate the individual with the culture, which makes possible potentially a new mind-set that will help us to live more fully in the 21st century.

The research is compelling and persuasive about the causal links between self-knowledge, psychological and physical well-being, and academic achievement. Numerous studies from the psychological and medical professions demonstrate the direct causal relationship between self-esteem and depression and obesity, having a purpose in life and emotional well-being, and self-efficacy and positive life-course trajectories (Bandura et al., 2001; CDC, 2012; Cohen, 2006; Goetz et al., 2003; Locker and Cropley, 2004; Mann et al., 2004; Orth et al., 2012; Ryan and Deci, 2000; Ryff and Singer, 1998a; 1998b; Ternouth et al., 2009).

Consider that all human beings go through numerous experiences that require having a solid foundation of self to draw upon to provide a prism and compass for overcoming impacts to our psyche, such as childhood sexual abuse, family divorce, job loss, and posttraumatic stress disorder (PTSD) from trauma experienced in life (and, for veterans, in combat) to name a few.

One particularly important research study, known as the ACE (Adverse Childhood Experiences) study, found interrelated and causal relationships between adverse childhood experiences, social-emotional and cognitive impairment, adverse or health risk behaviors, disease, disability and social problems, and life expectancy (Felitti et al., 1998; Felitti and Anda, 2009).

Numerous studies underscore the impact of poor self-esteem on a host of preventable illnesses. One study of 6,500 participants in England found that ten-year-olds with emotional problems who felt less in control of their lives were most likely to gain weight over the next twenty years, with girls affected more than boys. Professor and lead researcher Dr. Andrew Ternouth recommended that "early intervention for children suffering low self-esteem, anxiety, or other emotional challenges could help improve their changes of long-term physical health" and "strategies to promote social and emotional aspects of learning, including the promotion of self-esteem, are central to a number of recent policy initiatives" (Ternouth et al., 2009, p. 8).

Leading researchers from Europe and Australia, where, in our view, they are ahead of the United States in their thinking about well-being, found: "Self-esteem is an important risk and protective factor linked to a diversity of health and social outcomes. Therefore, self-esteem enhancement can serve as a key component in an integrated student success approach in prevention and health promotion. The design and implementation of mental health programs with self-esteem as one of the core variables is an important and promising development in health promotion" (Mann, Hosman, Schaalma, and de Vries, 2004, p. 368).

According to another important study on the importance of self-esteem when developing psychologically from adolescence to young adulthood, "growth curve analyses indicated that self-esteem increases from adolescence to middle adulthood, reaches a peak at about age 50 years, and then decreases in old age" (Orth, Robbins, and Widaman, 2012, p. 1), underscoring the need to teach self-knowledge. Further, this same study found strong correlations between self-esteem and strong relationships, professional career success, and job satisfaction and health. One can conclude that it is best to foster high self-esteem from childhood through adolescence and adulthood as a protective factor for a positive life course. We encourage front line educators to adopt the lens of the self in order to more deeply impact their students' ability to create a positive life course trajectory from eighteen to fifty. Students will know where they received this valuable framework with which to design their life, leading to a long-term positive relationship with their college or university.

With the growing and compelling researched-based evidence pointing to the correlations between self-esteem and health, and a life filled with success, it is ethically and morally the right thing to teach self-knowledge through our system of education; this can be achieved by integrating the student success functions in our model.

We have dedicated our lives to studying and empowering the self from numerous perspectives in order to transform students' lives and their experiences through schooling. In our K-16 teaching, higher education leadership, and counseling practice, we have worked with clients seeking guidance to choose a college, change careers, conquer substance abuse, overcome marriage and family dysfunction, and recover from sexual abuse, and numerous DSM-V diagnoses.

The one common denominator that we have found in all cases is that the pathway to success—whether it be academic and career success, emotional and psychological healing, or inner peace and love—is through a better understanding of one's self and making one's self and self-knowledge a high priority.

Student-Centered Education

Students want us to help them integrate all their dimensions, all their needs into a holistic view of who they are and how to succeed. University leaders want to be more effective at helping students achieve well-being and through the integration of organizational functions. And those professionals working hard in each of the functions want an integrated set of tools to help them achieve new levels of professional effectiveness.

In our view higher education can do more to help students learn about themselves as the most important factor in creating a happy, healthy, and flourishing life, and therefore a better world. Students are demanding more and more assistance to help them figure out who they are and how to be better and more successful people in order to make their unique impact in a world filled with problems that will require their best efforts and their best selves.

We need to envision a transformed system of higher education that can support learners in gaining self-knowledge for personal and professional potential, so they can demonstrate real competencies and succeed in life.

The context of higher education is changing because our students are changing. Students are required to navigate their own learning experiences through multiple curricula available in their institutions. Baxter Magolda's (2010) work demonstrating that self-authorship leads to successful careers is relevant in that she documented a student's growth of consciousness through a four-year education (Kegan, 1999). She found that students are required to create meaning from a complex set of experiences gained through the delivered curriculum, lived curriculum, and experienced curriculum (Yancy, 2004). These findings lead us to consider student success as measured from a holistic perspective, defined by students themselves. The students themselves become the center of their college learning experiences, where they create their own pathways to success.

The research on more holistic approaches to student success has been demonstrated to produce the following results:

- Knowing oneself leads to a sense of control and positive emotions that are essential to psychological well-being (Baumgardner, 1990, p. 1070).

- Students are likely to perform at a higher level when they feel they have some kind of academic "destination" in mind—or at least when they feel that what they are doing will lead to such a trajectory (Pintrich, quoted in Sternberg, 2013).
- Students with higher levels of well-being outperform those with lower levels of well-being, earning, on average, 10 percent more credits and a 2.9 GPA, versus completing fewer credits and a 2.4 GPA (Lopez, 2011, p. 2).
- Self-knowledge is the number one protective factor for a positive life course trajectory (Brzycki, 2013).

With a comprehensive student success program, along with a set of best practices, students can put together their own success pathways and merge their college experiences into a sense of personal meaning.

Students are seeking deeper meaning, personally and professionally, for their learning careers and for life.

Today's college students are seeking a model or approach to life that will provide for personalized pathways to a good life, a successful life.

Learning through the Lens of the Self

To achieve the highest vision for our society, we need to start with each individual, one person at a time.

Educators need to place the student at the center of his or her own educational experiences. The self then becomes the lens through which student learning takes place. This lens is the nexus of learning across all contexts: academic learning in a classroom setting; academic advising by faculty and professional advisors; cocurricular and extracurricular student engagement opportunities, career counseling, and internships; and CAPS. Our formula for student success is

$$\text{Student success} = \text{Intellectual growth} + \text{Individual development}$$
$$\text{Individual development} = \text{Well-being} + \text{Self-knowledge}$$

Therefore, intellectual and academic achievement represents only a part of student success. College students in today's higher education environment are increasingly required to navigate their own learning through a combination of understanding their own unique needs and seeking out those opportunities presented through their college or university. In order to know their unique needs, students require a framework or model from which to know and understand themselves. If we have this framework, then interactions between students and advisors, students and faculty, and students and counselors will improve integrative learning outcomes.

People need a new way of looking at who they are and their world, a new mind-set. This new mind-set desperately needed by students and society in general today is one based on our human potential and our abilities to know ourselves deeply and create ourselves anew over our life-spans. If individual well-being or a whole person's happiness is the foci, then productive, creative, emotionally competent people will emerge from our system of higher education—people possessing the attributes we need to make our organizations, communities, families, and society better. To create a better society, better citizens, better family members, and better workers, we need to create better people first.

We can and should teach college students that what is inside themselves is the most direct pathway to building a better society and workforce through better people. We are increasing the social and human capital through education in a very direct manner: Each person can improve our society and has a special and unique role and responsibility to do so. We are being called to change society for the better, and if we teach students what is inside them, which is the real driver of economic and cultural change and achievement, we will change the paradigm to meet the human needs of our time.

To respond to this need, to change the paradigm of education, we have developed a breakthrough new model called *Integrated Student Success (iSuccess)*. The "i" in the name represents the model's integration of each student's self-knowledge, placing the student's unique mind-set at the center of success. The "i" also represents the integration of the higher education functional areas that support students—academic advising, career services, personal counseling, faculty teaching, and student engagement. In this chapter, we introduced the core concept of *iSuccess*—that student success stems from well-being and self-knowledge. We build upon the *iSuccess* model throughout the remainder of the book.

Final Thoughts

Self-knowledge provides a pathway to full potential—academic and personal—that will help universities focus on whole person well-being. In the words of psychologist James Hillman (1996; 1999), "We want people to envision that what children go through has to do with finding a place in the world for their specific calling [purpose and potential in life]. They are trying to live two lives at once, the one they were born with and the one of the place and among the people they were born into" (Hillman, 1996, p. 13).

With compelling evidence making the direct connection between self-esteem and mental and physical well-being, we hope that this book inspires action by higher education policy makers, education leaders, and practitioners alike to reshape our educational system with a new sense of focus on the self and the paramount importance of the individual in the establishment of well-being and, in turn, wellness in society as a whole.

CHAPTER 3

HIGHER EDUCATION'S NEW MISSION

Both college students and frontline college educators are becoming increasingly aware that we need to shift from simply protecting students from harm to developing psychologically healthy and stronger people as a part of the educational mission. Higher education needs to embed practices that impart self-knowledge in all student success functional areas. Educators need to do this in a seamless and integrated way that does not always require students to enroll in separate specialized programs, potentially missing the opportunity to develop themselves and their pathways to success throughout every college experience.

Colleges and universities and the professional organizations that support them are making strides toward aligning student success with well-being in order to meet the needs of today's students. While we believe there are many improvements to be made moving forward toward fully embracing the core principles of our *iSuccess* model, there has been progress made in recent years showing that higher education may soon be ready to fully embrace its new mission and responsibilities to better serve today's students.

Integrating Well-Being into Student Success Functions

Dr. Larry Marks, a licensed psychologist in the counseling and psychological services department at the University of Central Florida, and Dr. John Wade, an associate professor at Emporia State University, are applying positive psychology to higher education. They put into perspective why universities should include well-being attributions as a part of their institutional student functions: "Focusing on personal strengths, positive emotions, wellbeing, and factors related to success and thriving can connect with an inner sense of hope and an uplifting desire for growth and constructive change. Indeed, there is a congruency between these concepts of positive psychology and the focus on growth, acquiring knowledge and skills, and nurturing of talent and potential that defines higher education. Furthermore, we have found that a positive psychology approach, including focusing on well-being and goal achievement, is often experienced as motivating and is well received by students" (Marks and Wade, 2015, p. 10).

When frontline educators create the environment for well-being and self-knowledge, they help further the purpose of higher education—to develop happy, healthy, flourishing, successful people who can realize their unique potentials in service to our common good.

The traditional cognitive functions that universities are accustomed to developing cannot be separated from the noncognitive functioning of the whole student, nor as Marks and Wade demonstrated, separated from positive psychology attributions such as hope, positive emotions, and motivation.

The foundational work of humanistic psychologists Abraham Maslow (1954; 1968) and Carl Rogers (1961; 1989) helped create a paradigm shift from mental illness to mental health, which is the focus of positive psychology and of this book. Their contemporary Marie Jahoda (1958) provided a framework for understanding the conceptual distinctions of mental health applied to higher education. The six processes that contribute to mental health are

1. Acceptance of oneself
2. Growth/development/becoming
3. Integration of personality
4. Autonomy
5. Accurate perception of reality
6. Environmental mastery

All six of these processes are developed and learned through higher education and are critical student success factors for a positive life-course trajectory.

Feeling Engaged

A 2014 poll by Gallup and Purdue University of more than 30,000 US college graduates revealed that those who rated their engagement in college and the support that they perceived from the institution as high were more likely to be currently engaged at work and thriving in areas of well-being compared to those who rated their college engagement and support as low. Especially notable was that this finding was consistent across all sizes and types of higher education institutions, lending evidence to the significant impact of experiencing well-being during college.

We have found that the most effective way to engage students in their college learning careers is by "teaching students about well-being and success and creating the conditions across various campus venues for enhancing well-being. . . . [This] adds value to their college experience and prepares them to be successful throughout life" (Mark and Wade, 2015, p. 14). For numerous reasons, from high-minded social responsibility to institutional business priorities to simply a desire to assist people in need, placing well-being at the center of our students' success works.

These interdisciplinary perspectives offer important insights into the need for a comprehensive model of self in higher education and a new integrated student success model.

As we teach numerous distinctions about the self in our classrooms, young adults should emerge from their schooling experiences more able to be well, with a greater understanding of what it means to be healthy—emotionally, physically, spiritually, intellectually, and psychologically.

Academic learning and success needs to stem from student well-being and contribute to it, rather than being the sole purpose of college or occurring without regard to larger humanistic concerns. All too often, scholars only think deeply and thoroughly about their particular fields of expertise, rarely daring to cross over into another body of knowledge at the risk of marginalizing their influence and reputations that take so long to build. The same silo can exist in the five critical student success functional areas: academic advising, career counseling, counseling and psychological services (CAPS), faculty teaching, and student engagement.

With the world changing rapidly and growing in complexity, our students, those young adults in our care, need us to think in new ways and, more directly, to teach them how to think about their personal pathways to their vision for success. We need to think about our problems from numerous perspectives and draw upon the best insights from each in order to create a breakthrough in our abilities to solve many acute problems. We need an interdisciplinary view to solve problems—to hopefully create a breakthrough that will empower humanity to be better, in a way that is consistent with our highest visions for what is possible.

Student Success Activities

According to comprehensive survey done by The Chronicle of Higher Education (Selingo, 2015), most institutions of higher education report that they are engaged in eighteen student success activities. These activities are typically managed under different institutional functions, and colleges and universities have not shared best practices to enhance each of these activities, nor developed a unifying model to connect them all to maximize their effectiveness. As a natural consequence, tuitions will increase in order to provide more of these services, and more professionals will be added to staff and administer these.

The eighteen student success activities are

1. Orientation
2. Academic tutoring or coaching
3. Intervention alert system
4. Writing or study skills program
5. Degree planning
6. Professional advising
7. First-year programs
8. Freshman seminars
9. Living and learning communities
10. Faculty instructional development
11. Career exploration programs
12. Summer bridge programs
13. Mentoring programs
14. Placement and assessment programs
15. Monitoring of gateway courses
16. Intrusive advising
17. Programs to improve student awareness of key services
18. Midterm academic progress alerts

We are offering a student success model that adds value to these student success activities by infusing them with high-impact practices that integrate the activities and convey self-knowledge. We suggest professional development training for those professionals in all five student success functions using the *iSuccess* model. The advantages are many: First, departments and units will reduce training costs for their particular areas of expertise. Second, each function and all professionals will have a common language to speak about students' needs. Third, each function and all professionals will have a set of high-impact student success practices, thereby increasing their effectiveness when supporting students. Finally, there will be more seamless collaboration among functions, with the amelioration of departments and battles for control and power.

Our model encourages the development of higher education, student success professionals who work in these five functions: academic advising, career counseling, CAPS, faculty teaching, and student engagement. Currently, there are best practices used in each of these; sometimes there are shared practices, but too few. The student success, *iSuccess* model places the holistic needs of students at the center and integrates all five functions into a seamless whole.

The professionals in these five functions know their fields and how to be effective. However, when we consult with higher education institutions about how to transform the student experience during their learning careers, we often find that institutions want to be able to help students more holistically and with deeper impact. They know that students need more supports that provide meaningful and integrated results beyond additional tutoring, more advising sessions about which courses qualify for a particular major, more online self-directed videos about sleep or anxiety from CAPS, and additional resume writing workshops from career services. These services all come from the five student success functions separately, not consistently integrated or coordinated in the theoretical basis of one model. The additional services that students need require a common approach, a model that provides a lens for both students and professionals.

We want frontline educators to be more able to see new connections between and among the five functions, and to deepen their understanding of how to apply self-knowledge in each of the student success functions. We also want educators to gain an appreciation at varying levels for producing well-being outcomes as mission critical. This does not require becoming a licensed counseling psychologist, but rather awareness of the *iSuccess* model.

Students' Personal Definitions of Success

How will colleges and universities change in order to meet these increased needs as well as produce successful alumni who feel a deep connection to their institution? The standard metric of simply helping students get through their course work and graduate no longer works. Students need more.

Dr. Thomas Grites, Assistant Provost at Stockton University, has provided leadership to the academic advising profession for more than thirty years, making important contributions by advocating for a "developmental model" to advising and working with students. He understands that students are seeking more from their higher education experiences in terms of personal, professional, and academic experiences—a holistic view. We are fortunate he provided us with his unique perspective in a personal communication via e-mail (March 2016):

> The standard metric for student success—completion—is still prominent, and clearly remains very important for American higher education. However, it appears that several advocates for alternative definitions and characteristics of student success are becoming more visible and might just create enough awareness among all the higher education stakeholders that other outcomes should not be neglected. Perhaps institutions should invest more efforts to determine all newly enrolled students' aspirations and goals as the criteria for success, acknowledge "the X factor," and develop metrics . . . to determine whether their students have been successful. Wouldn't fulfilling one's aspirations and reaching one's goals be wonderful "student success" statistics to promote? It would also greatly reduce my search efforts, yet re-assure me that our students are being successful—in their own purposeful ways.

The student success model should represent a set of metrics from students' perspectives.

We can agree that no matter how you measure student success, completion rates, or well-being, higher education needs a new perspective, another way of looking at how educators are supporting students, a new integrated model.

Integrated and Interdisciplinary

Integrative learning, a growing framework for building an integrated set of best practices and one advocated by the Association of American Colleges and Universities (AAC&U), creates a context for numerous college units or departments to focus on students' needs, and provides a student-centered approach that cuts across disciplines.

Our student success model is interdisciplinary in that it connects five key higher education functions through a student-centered and student-defined or authored success. In addition, it integrates a seamless set of practices across functions. Because students have self-interest in learning about who they are, we use our integrated self model in order to give students a reference point in self-authorship.

The Carnegie Foundation's work on integrated learning also considers the central role of self-knowledge in higher education: "The idea of making students more self-aware and purposeful—more intentional—about their studies is a powerful one, and it is key to fostering integrative learning" (Taylor, Huber, and Hutchings, 2004, p.16). The University of Michigan exemplifies the application of the AAC&U integrative learning framework by effectively combining several key student success functions into the office of student life (University of Michigan, 2016).

Students today face growing pressure to pursue higher education, with the end goal of being prepared for a career. Yet one of the greatest challenges in higher education is that many degrees were not designed for this purpose. Instead, the curriculum was (and is) designed to provide students with an opportunity to learn to think, and the best learning situations "foster students' abilities to integrate their learning across contexts and over time" (Huber and Hutchings, 2004).

Our student success model provides students with a way to understand who they are as learners and the ways in which they have developed their ability to integrate their learning experiences for use in their personal, professional, and civic life.

Trends toward Integration

California State University System (2016) promotes student self-efficacy and identity formulation through their outreach to faculty In 2016, they allocated $7.2 million for student success programs that included workshops by faculty on how students can develop self-efficacy. Additionally CSU offers workshops for faculty on how to extend classroom learning to the community through service learning activities. As a result of implementing this type of high-impact learning, six-year graduation rates for Latino students have increased from 38 percent to 65 percent over a three-year period, and 55 percent to 68 percent for non-Latino students.

To demonstrate the growing importance of including student success initiatives in your institution's mission, St. Petersburg College in Florida states that its mission is to "promote student success and enrich our communities through education, career development, and self-discovery."

St. Petersburg College's model (2015) is oriented around their students and their commitment to them, and to applying all resources toward helping students understand what success means. All employees, faculty, and staff are required to take special training in how they can support student success through *The College Experience* program.

Even though St. Petersburg College keeps numerous institutional statistics on student success, we would like to see this college develop even more advanced metrics that indicate different aspects of "self-discovery" based on the Ryff or other psychological well-being scales to be more thoroughly consistent with their mission and be more genuinely student centered.

In Cornell's strategic plan, the university made it a priority and responsibility to teach coping or life skills to their students as a part of the academic mission, asserting this as "the obligation of the university." "While we maintain and nurture the existing strengths of Cornell's student experience, improving teaching, enhancing the diversity of the student body, and nurturing student health and well-being are priorities" (Cornell University, 2015).

As a demonstration of this commitment to "nurturing student health and well-being," Cornell's Gannett Health Services Center imparts the attribute of "resilience" in the areas of cognitive, behavioral, motivational, existential/spiritual, relational, and emotional stress, with the intent that this characteristic will enhance a student's overall success and carry forward beyond life at Cornell. We feel that the work being done in the Gannett Center at Cornell University represents the appropriate integration of well-being with academics in support of student success, and establishes appropriate organizational functions in support of their mission. Cornell is excelling.

Promoting Resilience

Resilience is an individual's ability to positively cope with stress and adversity, "bouncing back" to a previous state of normal functioning, or using the experience of adversity to enhance flexibility and overall functioning. Resilience has multidimensional aspects (Wong, 2012), including the following (Cornell Gannett Health Services, 2016):

- *Cognitive.* How events are interpreted (cognitive style, appraisal, attribution) and how daily stressors and life circumstances are negotiated (coping)
- *Behavioral.* Habits of persistence and endurance in face of obstacles and failures (behavioral practice and reinforcement)
- *Motivational.* Clear sense of life purpose and commitment (will to live)
- *Existential/spiritual.* Sense of larger purpose and meaning of human life (meaning and life purpose)

- *Relational.* Sense of social connectedness, engagement, and altruism
- *Emotional.* Ability to tolerate negative emotions and rejection and to maintain emotional confidence and hopefulness (emotion regulation, emotional intelligence)

Resilience stems from the interaction of a person with their environment and the resulting processes that either promote well-being or protect them against the overwhelming influence of risk factors. One of the best ways people build resilience is through interaction with others. These processes can be helped along by experiences in families, colleges/universities, and other social communities that help individuals learn how to productively confront adversity (Cornell Gannett Health Services, 2016).

Our research found a wide difference between schools that are proactively supporting student resilience and those that have not even considered shifting to a student success focus, either strategically or through new programs and organizational functions.

Student Success Centers

Wright State University's new model implemented in June 2015 includes bringing together the university functions typically associated with student success. They have recently launched a student success center that combines tutoring, academic advising, and study spaces in one location. Further, they use data capture technology to determine if students are attending classes or the success center, so as to achieve the institutional goals of graduation or completion rates.

However, if the student success center at Wright State and elsewhere used a set of tools that help students understand and define their own success, then we assert students would not require so many remedial, labor intensive supports such as academic tutoring, and universities might not need to allocate so many resources toward these external supports. Certainly, student self-authorship of success pathways would help enhance the effectiveness of the center.

The Center at Wright State, while laudable, appears to place emphasis on supports that do not impact the inner selves of their students, which would expand their effectiveness at a time of limited capacity.

First-Year Programs

Dr. Joshua Wilkin, Associate Director for Student Life at Bryant University, is attempting to improve the experiences of college students as reported in the student opinion survey (SOS). He is aware of the importance of making certain that specific positive psychology attributes are included in first-year programs and those throughout a student's four years. In his recent study (2016), he found his students wanted more of a sense of belonging.

He referred to a study by Morrow and Ackerman (2012), who investigated the importance of motivation and sense of belonging as they relate to retention. The authors sought to find out if increased levels of peer support, faculty support, classroom comfort, intrinsic value, instrumental value, and personal development would be related to self-reported intention to persist into the student's second year of study. The authors conducted a study at a PhD-granting institution with 156 students and found that high levels of faculty support, peer support, personal development, and motivation meant students were more inclined to return their sophomore year. Additionally, Dr. Wilkin found evidence for taking a new approach from the student's perspective when a wellness model was utilized. Choate and Smith (2003) took a related approach and researched the impact first-year experience programs had on a wellness model that was implemented at a small private institution in the Southeast. Results indicated that the wellness model enhanced student learning through increasing self-awareness, self-direction, recognition of the interrelatedness of all life areas, the identification of strengths and areas for improvement, and appreciation of strategies for change.

Clearly, any model of student success needs to take an interdisciplinary or integrative perspective, while placing the student's perspective and well-being needs at the center.

Dr. Wilkin's research affirms the importance of first-year programs that place students' developmental needs first:

> Overwhelmingly, 29 out of 30 participants indicated a first-year experience course or seminar would enhance a student's first-year experience and address the gaps of social support and communication at the college. Participants felt this course or seminar should continue throughout the year and provide increased programmatic opportunities for students to engage socially and academically. Participants felt this course or seminar could assist students' developmental growth by working with them to improve their social interactions, manage stress and time management more efficiently as well as adapt to difficult situations. Participants shared that the course or seminar needed

to show students how to use all the support services the college offers. Many shared that students needed to learn about having access to the counseling center for emotional support, writing studio for academic support, advisement center for course selection support, and health services for physical care. (2016, p. 18)

Top universities with visionary leadership supporting their students' success realize first-year programs strengthen the entire college experience and extend to a lifelong relationship. This demonstrates to prospective students, current students, and alumni that the institution cares about their well-being from matriculation to graduation—for life.

High Stakes

In 2014–15, the University of Pennsylvania experienced six suicides in a fourteen month period. A special task force put forth a set of recommendations to address "the challenges confronting students that can affect their psychological health and wellbeing; review and assess the efficacy of Penn resources for helping students manage psychological problems, stress, or situational crises; and make recommendations related to programs, policies, and practices designed to improve the quality and safety of student life" (2015).

This University of Pennsylvania report underscores the importance of student wellness and taking care of oneself while on campus and beyond, with the following recommendations:

- Communicating at every level of the student experience about the importance of mental health and wellbeing to student success
- Making information about available resources and supports for student mental health and wellness across the university easily accessible
- Educating and training faculty, staff, students, parents, and families about fostering mental health and responding to students who need help
- Optimizing the resources devoted to CAPS to meet the needs of students as efforts continue to engage the entire community in sustaining and improving the psychological health and well-being of Penn students

It is critical in our view that university leaders relay to students the interconnectedness among mental health and well-being to student success. From new student orientation sessions, to enrolling into classes, to the first day of classes, students need to understand what frontline educators have come to know about how to succeed in college and life.

Frontline educators require a set of tools, however, to be more able to teach students about well-being as central to success—especially given our expanded definition of well-being that is based on state of the art psychology with the latest innovations and approaches.

The University of Pennsylvania indicates, "Responsibility for fostering student success and wellbeing goes far beyond the institutional programs that have been instituted. Every student at Penn has a network of support, official and unofficial, that spans friends, family, peers, peer educators, academic advisors, faculty, and staff in student services and other roles. Students (undergraduate, graduate, and professional) are expected to take responsibility for their own wellbeing" (2015, p. 2). We agree with this statement and believe it could apply to all institutions of higher education,

We find it heartening to see a growing recognition that student success and wellness go hand in hand, that they are inextricably linked. Additionally, there is a growing understanding that the competitiveness found on our college campuses and so too in our modern society is a risk factor to success on campus and in life. These risk factors begin all too early for some—research has shown that half of all mental illness begins prior to age fourteen. This compels us to help students develop a new mind-set, one that will help ameliorate these risk factors and stressors, leading to a happy, healthy, flourishing life. This new mind-set can be learned, and should be learned, in our educational institutions, which are most responsible for providing the necessary knowledge for a good life. We have dedicated the past thirty years of our lives to developing tools and a set of student success high-impact practices that impart attributions to thrive in our modern society.

The Gap between Prevention and Treatment

When educators, advisors, and counselors talk about well-being, they too often only look at treatment and not prevention.

Take, for example, the recent development at the university level to address the well-being of eighteen- to twenty-five-year-old young adults in their college educational experiences by hiring a well-being professional. See this employment listing from a highly competitive private liberal arts college in the Northeast for a director of health and wellness education: "[The] College is seeking qualified candidates for a new position in our Dean of Students office. The Director of Health and Wellness Education will develop, implement and evaluate a broad-based health and wellness education program with a focus on alcohol and drug use, sexual assault prevention and response, stress management, and bystander intervention programs" (HigherEdJobs.com).

We have observed that most wellness education programs are likely reactions to mental and physical health crises, with a focus on alcohol and drug use, sexual assault, and stress management. If frontline educators in our student success functional areas are teaching young adults self-knowledge and how to create a paradigm shift in their abilities to experience life and create the life of their calling, we would then teach preventatively during college how to find inner peace and understanding when faced with the stressors of modern life. The emphasis could be placed on teaching self-knowledge as a significant protective factor for use over one's life-span.

Well-being education is an important prevention strategy for all colleges and universities to formulate and implement. More directly, students (and their parents) should demand innovative programs that impart well-being attributions as part of their broader college experiences.

In a job ad for a prestigious mid-Atlantic liberal arts university, we see the gap reflected in policies regarding resources allocated toward treatment versus prevention. This position description speaks to many preventative policies and visions but then describes duties and responsibilities that focus primarily on treatment (HigherEdJobs.com):

> In support of the university's commitment to the development of self-aware, emotionally stable, socially responsible and productive citizens, the university seeks to
> 1. Enhance students' psychological development, including intellectual, emotional, and physical self-awareness and growth.
> 2. Improve students' interpersonal skills and understanding of their personal roles, responsibilities, and contributions to relationships and to a diverse and vibrant university community.
> 3. Assist students to develop a healthy integrated lifestyle that accommodates new perspectives and diverse ideas and that are responsive to change and challenges.
> 4. Help students cope with and overcome psychological difficulties or obstacles to their academic success and personal satisfaction.
> 5. Support students in psychological crisis to regain psychological health and develop effective coping skills.
> 6. Provide students with a safe, inclusive, and confidential environment in which they are heard, affirmed, and encouraged to explore and learn about themselves and their life experiences.

7. Enhance the university's understanding of college mental health issues and collaborate with members of the community to address student needs and concerns.
8. Model a professional lifestyle that balances professional practice, professional development, and professional and personal fulfillment.

In our view, these job responsibilities represent our highest hopes and vision for all institutions of higher education (or IHEs), especially in regard to *prevention*.

However, in addition to planning, budgeting oversight, staff coordination, record keeping, maintaining policies, and committee work, this job's duties and responsibilities primarily address mental health responses, procedures, and protocols, with a clear focus on *treatment*:

Duties and Responsibilities
- Provide leadership and vision for the [university unit] by creating a culture of high-quality care and continuous improvement.
- Ensure efficient, equitable, and quality delivery of all clinical services, including assessment, individual, and group counseling, referral, consultation, and crisis intervention.
- Provide direct clinical service including individual and group counseling, assessment, crisis intervention, and consultation.
- Provide clinical oversight, consultation, and leadership in supporting students who present a danger to themselves and/or others and share necessary communication when ethically and legally appropriate.
- Oversee assessment efforts addressing both needs assessment and outcome evaluations.
- Foster strong professional relationships with local mental health providers for referral and networking.
- Ensure full compliance with mental health ethical standards, including maintaining confidential client records, data, and all [state] licensure requirements.

Note the use of language that leans toward treatment versus prevention: "assessment, crisis intervention . . . supporting students who present a danger to themselves and/or others." University-based mental health and well-being services too often lean in the direction of treatment, including the use of multiple assessments. A truly preventative approach would embed self-development educational programming into the ongoing and key university functions that make up student success supports.

Certainly, this university is not unique in attempting to address such large problems of student well-being and flourishing from the mind-set of treatment versus prevention. This is the medical model that is so prominent in our society, one that has caused the Centers for Disease Control and Prevention (Haegerich et al. 2016) to come out with a new report advising that Americans cannot simply continue to live their current lifestyles by upping their doses of medications.

Prevention in our view does not simply come from early diagnosis through assessments. Our work proactively prevents mental illness by giving students the tools that they need to construct a self, a healthy self, thereby ameliorating any symptoms that may arise due to adverse childhood experiences or other factors.

Mental health has been identified as a significant issue facing higher education. Framing mental health as mental illness has yielded treatment-centered services overwhelmed with demand. Reframing mental health as capacities for flourishing and student success can generate new approaches that enhance mental health and wellness among all students. We advocate for reframing mental health as well-being, which reflects the influence of positive psychology.

If colleges and universities continue to follow this strategy—of throwing more money at CAPS positions so to impact the mental health and well-being of students as an integral strategy to student success without making the shift from mental illness treatment to well-being protective factors, then this becomes a never-ending money pit. Students want student success services to make an impact on who they are, to help them increase their ability to understand themselves at the deepest levels, and to teach them how to create their own destinies in life through everyday associated activities and programs. Students want to learn how to be self-directed and have self-responsibility, but they have been brought up to be very dependent on outside supports, instead of first looking inward.

Returning to Penn State as an example from Chapter 1 of the challenges IHEs face, the vice-president of student affairs declared at a publicly-held board of trustees meeting recently, "CAPS is receiving higher incidences of anxiety and depression," with "more so than usual behavior issues, where needs continue to grow each year and there is a long growing waiting list." He concluded, "We are not going to find enough money to remedy the situation."

This is a sad commentary that expresses the depth of resignation among college and university leaders that anything can be done to reverse such a troubling situation.

At Penn State, there has been a 33 percent increase in the number of students treated through CAPS over the past five years—an additional three thousand students—during a time where enrollment went up by only 5 percent. To attempt to meet the growing demand, the university is experimenting with a new model of embedding counselors in residence halls. According to the executive director of CAPS, the goals are to further sensitize students and to reduce the stigma associated with participating in counseling. Does this go far enough? Other colleges and universities we have researched are taking an active role in promoting a set of preventative services and student-centered educational approaches that impart promising and high-impact practices. They understand that they can prevent incidences of mental health and impart well-being protective factors instead of only providing treatment.

A senior at Penn State said that mental health and well-being are "issue[s] that affect everyone around us," expressing the ubiquity of the issue on college campuses. We would like to see a new focus on adopting models of empowering students' well-being as a key strategy to address the swell of demand for services and to provide students with student success high-impact practices that transform their college experiences. Students understand the scope and depth of the issue of well-being, frontline higher educators want to help, and university leaders are struggling with how to implement the necessary changes.

What is needed in all higher education institutions is a framework like the *iSuccess* model, which offers a single student-centered pedagogy, and high-impact practices that transform the positive life course trajectory of every student. Impacting students' positive life course trajectory means transforming students' learning careers and college experiences—and not only offering service centers where students seek assistance after problems arise and often have to wait to get the support they need.

We met with a college senior who had a stellar academic record, leadership positions in her sorority and campus philanthropy, and partially supported herself financially through a part-time job. By all accounts, she was someone who has been successful in her college learning career. We met with her to discuss her plans for after college. She had not met with the professionals in one of the highest rated career services offices in the country (Wall Street Journal Survey, 2010). She was struggling with what to do after college and did not have a framework to think about this issue. She felt lost and directionless, and was becoming more and more resentful that she did not get the type of advice needed to help her establish her direction. For this student, just following the rules established for students in her university were not enough to provide her with what she needed, which was a stronger sense of self-efficacy and self-determination that she was in charge of her destiny in life and could do something about it.

At present, CAPS at most IHEs is too separate from the everyday functions that support student success. We are recommending that CAPS be more integrated and integral across all five student success functions.

Gap between Mission and Practice

It is in the interest and to the advantage of leaders of today's colleges and universities to be constantly growing and anticipating changing student needs. Some researchers, academics, and administrators realize that changes need to be made, and they are providing the leadership to implement the necessary changes.

But even though we have highlighted a few universities who have begun to transform their cultures around student success, generally higher education is moving slowly toward a student-centered, integrated, preventative student success model.

Many institutions of higher education are not able to keep up with demand for counseling and psychological services, and do not have a comprehensive solution or approach for doing so. Therefore, IHEs have a growing gap between their bold strategic initiatives or mission statements and the actual organizational changes and student success programming required to realize their goals. Many universities that have not made the systemic and organizational changes required to transform to this new student success model and thereby meet the changing needs of students. They are still stuck in the divide between student affairs and academic affairs (often governed by faculty senate policies). For example, Penn State, in its strategic plan for 2016 to 2020, makes it a visionary thematic priority to address health and well-being, saying it will "Facilitate wellness within the Penn State community. Because our University is only as strong as its people, we will invest in innovative, multi-pronged, institution-wide health initiative that inspires faculty, staff, and students to focus proactively on their physical, mental, and emotional wellness. The effort across all Penn State campuses will encourage faculty, staff, and students alike to pursue recommended preventative health care services and educate them about behaviors (such as physical activity, healthy eating and drinking, smoking prevention and cessation, and stress management) that experts agree promote health and prolong life"(Penn State, 2016, p. 10). Yet, as we have seen in our previous discussions, like many other IHEs, Penn State is not fully able to meet the demand for mental health and well-being services and is struggling to find solutions.

In our research, we found that the Ohio State University (OSU) provides leadership to the student success field by connecting actual solutions that match its mission statement. Here is an example from their 2015 Office of Student Life Wellness Assessment: "Student wellness is an essential component of academic success in higher education and subsequent opportunities in the labor market. Yet wellness itself has many facets. The Ohio State University Office of Student Life's Student Wellness Center uses a model that includes nine key dimensions of wellness: career, creative, emotional, environmental, financial, intellectual, physical, social and spiritual" (Ohio State, 2015). Ohio State is facilitating the integration of the student success functions, including career, academic, and personal advising, by integrating multiple dimensions of wellness in both the center's mission and structure. The Office of Student Life consists of over thirty departments that traditionally are very separate, including career counseling and support services, student wellness, student leadership and internships, and student advocacy (student advising), among others. The university also makes extensive use of wellness metrics to improve the lives of students during their learning career, while preparing them for life after college as productive, successful citizens in our society.

We see the increased need for academic affairs and student affairs organizations to be combined into one seamless whole in order to be better able to serve student needs. The student success model we are describing requires a higher contextual view of both, with new approaches and the elimination of outdated beliefs and practices that no longer serve the needs of modern students and society.

The time has come to move beyond developing high-level mission and vision statements about the importance of student success, mental health, and well-being, and put into place effective practices. How many deserving students and good people have passed through our ivy-covered walls only to go on and suffer in silence?

Implications

The *iSuccess* model calls for integrating the self *and* integrating the five institutional student success functions. Many colleges are making strides by offering programs or services that integrate an increased focus on the self, while others are integrating two or more functions. Very few IHEs do both.

There are organizational implications, cost considerations, and more that most institutions are not prepared to even think about, let alone address. But these considerations translate to improved student results and increased levels of satisfaction; thus these efforts are well worth the investment. The *iSuccess* model requires a new way of thinking by institutions as well as the key student success functions.

Here are some of the challenges that universities are facing that the *iSuccess* model can effect:

1. Growing and changing student needs that are becoming more holistic
2. Reduced application pools for traditional students, requiring new programming
3. Increased obstacles to degree completion due to modern stressors
4. Infusion of technology into delivery of academic programming and support of multiple campuses
5. Multiple campus locations all needing student services that align with academics for improved student results and lower costs to deliver services
6. Undefined leadership when coordinating all five student success functions

What do today's college students want? All students have complex, holistic needs that require the following supports:(1) the increased presence of a respected mentor;(2) deep and meaningful relationships with mentors; (3) socioemotional supports;(4) self-understanding and pathways for achieving potentials for success in school, career, and life; (5) the empowerment to realize they control their own destinies in life; (6) more real-world learning (RWL) opportunities; and (7) professional training toward a successful career and life. To provide these supports, we need new thinking, a new model, and student success high-impact practices.

Final Thoughts

To help students prepare to meet the increased psychological demands required in modern life, colleges must provide additional support—and not only from counseling professionals but also undergraduate advisers and faculty members.

IHEs need a new student success model that places students' needs at the center of all teaching and learning, counseling, advising, and engagement. The focus needs to shift from a narrow view limited to only retention rates, student satisfaction rates, or institutional needs. There is an unnecessary focus on institutional metrics that measure time to completion because of the costs associated with recruiting new students; our colleges and universities do not want students to drop out for loss of revenue, simply and harshly put. Further, state legislatures are releasing funds based on completion rates, fulfilling the states' needs, not student needs. We are not recommending a new student-focused lens only; however, student needs should be placed first or prioritized; only then should we consider the needs of the institutions and states.

Senior administrators need to view students, the academic advising relationship, and the broader college experience through a new lens that focuses much more on students' overall well-being and not just academics and traditional co-curricular and extracurricular activities alone. Today's faculty members and academic advisors are just not taught to think this way. They don't have a way to look at the problem, nor do they have a definition of what constitutes "well-being" to guide their prevention and education programs.

When a student's holistic needs, including well-being needs, are not met then they feel as though they are not getting what they came for—to know themselves more thoroughly and deeply, which serves as a protective factor to ensure lifelong success. Today's students are savvy and aware enough to know that success is a combination of factors made up of both cognitive and noncognitive factors and attributions. They expect educational institutions to equip them with the tools to become successful in college and in life.

We are making the argument that an increased focus on noncognitive factors can contribute more to student success than the present focus on cognitive factors alone—again, we do not want to exclude these important cognitive factors but raise the level of awareness and utilization of these factors across the myriad of student success functions.

When universities focus on a more appropriate and effective combination and balance between cognitive and noncognitive factors, students understand and learn a holistic model of who they are. Further, it takes the whole person to make it in life and establish a positive life course trajectory.

Higher education today requires a systematic process that helps students achieve their educational, career, and personal goals by concentrating on areas of talent and engagement, dreams and passions. Such a student success strategy will stimulate and support students in their quest for an enriched quality of life. This will, in turn, result in higher student satisfaction, increased retention and graduation rates, and at the most fundamental level, young adults who are fulfilled and psychologically healthy.

Higher education institutions of all types need to create new mission statements that specifically address the well-being of their students as a part of delivering their promise of a good life both during and after students' college careers. However, only a select few organizations have taken committed actions beyond mission statements to implement a broad-based student success strategy that includes student wellness. Higher education can no longer pass students onto adulthood with only degrees in academic subjects, but rather must provide strategies and practices that empower new dimensions of student success.

While student needs have changed, many higher education institutions have not kept pace, with a growing gap between espoused beliefs about students and high-impact practices that produce happy, healthy, flourishing students. Many institutions continue to think about well-being as simply protecting students from harm, rather than intentionally producing students with the self-knowledge to maintain lifelong wellness and success.

CHAPTER 4

STUDENT SUCCESS AND PROFESSIONAL STANDARDS

In this chapter we take a look at the standards of the professional organizations that serve the student success functions—academic advising, counseling and psychological services (CAPS), career counseling, faculty teaching—and select those standards that relate most directly to student success competencies. Of particular interest are competencies that directly relate to the *iSuccess* model. We underscore the changing and expanding definition of student success and the growing need for practices and new organizational alignments to produce successful outcomes from college learning careers.

Professional standards shape what is valued and important, and ultimately what is measured in higher education. Oftentimes these standards are used as a basis for accreditation of programs and as indicators of excellence. Additionally, professional associations are often out in front of their respective fields, establishing the future vision of what professionals can and should strive to achieve.

We feel a sense of partnership with the professional organizations that serve the five student success functions, because many of their standards focus on self-knowledge and the internal life of the student.

Student affairs organizations require professionals to view wellness as a broad concept, and to prepare students for "careers, citizenship, and lives" with a commitment to "integrity" and "spiritual awareness." Professionals are required to "facilitate reflection" and encourage "individual decision-making" and "holistic development." Academic advising organizations require professionals to respect "individual beliefs," gain insights into students' "personal experiences," foster "individual potential," and encourage "self-reliance" and "self-management." Career advising organizations refer to "positive self-concept," "self-assessment," and "self-regulation." Faculty organizations encourage the discernment of ethical consequences and the development of a "deep understanding of one's self."

As we review the standards that best support student success, we also argue that professionals need more methods, tools, and practices to help them manifest the standards and actually deliver results for students.

Periodically throughout this chapter, we have included comments in parentheses and italics to highlight connections between the standards presented and the *iSuccess* model for integrating the self through increased well-being and self-knowledge.

High-Impact Educational Practices

We begin by presenting what are commonly understood to be "high-impact educational practices" across all higher education endeavors. In a high-impact learning experience, students actively pose and solve problems, work collaboratively in a community of peers, experience real-world applications of knowledge, and reflect on their own learning processes (Kuh, 2008). According to the Association of American Colleges and Universities (following the work of George Kuh in *High-Impact Educational Practices: What They Are, Who Has Access to Them, and Why They Matter*), a number of educational experiences are conducive to high-impact learning, including:

- First-year seminars and experiences (*These include orientation sessions and short workshops on specific topics that will help students make a successful transition to college life.*)
- Common intellectual experiences (*A set of common courses explore themes and offer a variety of curricular and co-curricular activities.*)
- Learning communities (*These bring like-minded students together to explore a common topic across different disciplines, such as environmental issues or social justice.*)
- Writing-intensive courses (*These courses encourage students to write in a variety of forms across the curriculum and for final-year projects.*)
- Collaborative assignments and projects (*Students learn to listen to other perspectives by working to solve problems together.*)
- Undergraduate research (*Students in all disciplines and levels can participate in research projects to strengthen observational skills and deepen commitment to their chosen fields.*)

- Diversity and global learning (*Students explore different worldviews, inequality, and human rights through courses, programs, experiential learning, or study abroad.*)
- Service- or community-based learning (*This is a teaching and learning method that integrates critical reflection and meaningful service in the community with academic learning, personal growth, and civic responsibility.*)
- Internships (*These are real-world learning placements, both credit and noncredit, in organizations related to students' career interests.*)
- Capstone courses and projects (*Students create a paper, portfolio, or project that integrates and applies everything they have learned from their college experiences.*)

Kuh's high-impact practices have benefited students at numerous institutions and will offer even more opportunities for students if they are better integrated and systematized throughout these institutions. We must note that while these high-impact practices address numerous academic and cognitive skills and even noncognitive skills such as "commitment" and "personal growth," they need to more purposefully incorporate the noncognitive and self-knowledge focus we are advocating in our student success model. What is needed to make these practices truly effective is recognizing the student as a whole person who is participating in these practices, thereby making them more student centered. Student success professionals need a model or framework to understand the whole person who is experiencing each practice, as well as professional competencies that involve attributions of self that lead to student success. The practices espoused by Kuh (2008) can produce more impactful outcomes with the infusion and understanding of the self of each student.

Kuh identifies six elements common across the practices that, when employed, make practices more effective:

1. They are effortful. They "demand that students devote considerable time and effort to purposeful tasks [and] require daily decisions that deepen students' investment in the activity as well as their commitment to their academic program and the college."
2. They help students build substantive relationships and "interact . . . with faculty and peers about substantive matters . . . over extended periods of time" during which relationships develop that "put students in the company of mentors and advisers as well as peers who share intellectual interests and are committed to seeing that students succeed."
3. They help students engage across differences. High-impact practices help students "experience diversity through contact with people who are

different from themselves," and "challenge students to develop new ways of thinking about and responding immediately to novel circumstances as they work . . . on intellectual and practical tasks, inside and outside the classroom, on and off campus."

4. They provide students with rich feedback and frequent feedback, not limited to the assessment of classroom work but also including feedback from supervisors and colleagues.
5. They help students apply and test what they are learning in new situations and provide "opportunities for students to see how what they are learning works in different settings, on and off campus. These opportunities to integrate, symmetrize, and apply knowledge are essential to deep, meaningful learning experiences."
6. They provide opportunities for students to reflect on the person they are becoming. Reflection "deepen[s] learning and bring one's values and beliefs into awareness; [it] help[s] students develop the ability to take the measure of events and actions and put them in perspective. As a result, students better understand themselves in relation to others and the larger world, and they acquire the intellectual tools and ethical grounding to act with confidence for the betterment of the human condition."

Used with permission from Association of American Colleges and Universities (AAC&U).

Kuh's elements provide structure, goals, feedback, and relationships, but we would like to see more opportunities to explore the student's inner mindset. The sixth element directly addresses self-knowledge, which is the core of the *iSuccess* model, but while it mentions the betterment of the human condition, it does not address the student's own well-being as the starting point for that betterment.

The *iSuccess* model is a breakthrough because it brings self-knowledge and well-being to the center of higher education's mission. We propose that all of Kuh's practices and elements will be more meaningful and effective if self-knowledge and well-being come first.

ACPA and NASPA Student Success Standards

The American College Personnel Association (ACPA) and the National Association of Student Personnel Administrators (NASPA) have developed descriptions of competency areas that are "divided into basic, intermediate, and advanced levels that delineate the increasing complexity and ability that should be demonstrated by practitioners as they grow in their professional development" (ACPA and NASPA, 2010, p. 4).

ACPA broadly defines student affairs as "any advising, counseling, management, or administrative function at a college or university that exists outside the classroom." Department and program areas most often included in student affairs are "residence life, commuter services, graduate student services, admissions, new student orientation, financial aid, counseling centers, advising centers, leadership development, Greek affairs, student activities, student unions, leadership development, community service, service learning, career planning and placement, discipline and judicial affairs, alumni relations and development, services for students with disabilities, developmental learning services, and advocacy and support programs (e.g., for students of color, lesbian, bisexual, gay, and transgender students, veterans, women, international students, adults)" (2010). We view ACPA and NASPA as organizations for overarching student affairs professionals, while other organizations are more specialized to their field (e.g., career services).

The competency areas are (a) advising and helping; (b) assessment, evaluation, and research; (c) equity, diversity, and inclusion; (d) ethical professional practice; (e) history, philosophy, and values; (f) human and organizational resources; (g) law, policy, and governance; (h) leadership; (i) personal foundations; and (j) student learning and development (Hoffman and Bresciani, 2012).

Most critical and relevant to our student success model are the following descriptions, and we highlight specific key competencies that relate directly to student success.

The following standards have been used with permission by the ACPA and NASPA, from their 2010 *ACPA/NASPA Professional Competency Areas for Student Affairs Practitioners*.

Advising and Helping

The advising and helping competency area addresses the knowledge, skills, and attitudes related to providing counseling and advising support, direction, feedback, critique, referral, and guidance to individuals and groups.

- Facilitate reflection to make meaning from experience. (*The opportunity to be self-reflective enables one to think about life and one's place in it. To make meaning requires taking classroom concepts or advice from professional advisors and relating these to one's self, such as, "How does this relate to me and my life purpose and inform my dreams for my life?"*)

- Strategically and simultaneously pursue multiple objectives in conversations with students. (*Professional advisors engage in conversations about personal matters, well-being status, career options and direction, as well as academic program fit, among others, taking into consideration the holistic needs of students.*)
- Facilitate individual decision making and goal setting. (*Advisors and counselors coach students in such a manner that they are placed at the center of and responsible for making decisions about their future directions and the person they want to become. This is a student-centered approach.*)
- Identify when and with whom to implement appropriate crisis management and intervention responses. (*Advisors and counselors determine when to involve CAPS for expertise beyond an advisor's capabilities, with confidential sexual or alcohol abuse issues as examples.*)
- Actively seek out opportunities to expand one's own knowledge and skills in helping students with specific concerns. (*These concerns include, for example, suicidal students, depression, anxiety, and career advising models such as life management.*)
- Identify patterns of behavior that signal mental health concerns. (*These include self-harm, isolation, suppression of emotions, increased alcohol use, and lack of identity and self-understanding.*)
- Initiate crisis intervention responses and processes. (*Advisors and counselors use protocols for intrusive advising and/or referrals depending on crisis levels.*)
- Develop and implement successful prevention and outreach programs on campus, including effective mental health publicity and marketing. (*Expanded options include online therapy sessions, short-term workshops on personal issues, peer-to-peer counseling programs, and developing curricula for new student orientations and grade-to-grade transitions. Advisors and counselors can also work with faculty to embed well-being and self-knowledge distinctions across the curriculum.*)
- Develop and distribute accurate and helpful mental health information for students, faculty, and staff. (*CAPS and professional learning communities need to work together across campus.*)
- Develop avenues for student involvement in mental health promotion and destigmatization of mental illness. (*These avenues include creating student advisory councils, overseeing peer education programs, and advising student mental health organizations.*)

- Consult with mental health professionals as appropriate. (*Upon administering a well-being assessment instrument such as the* Success Predictor, *a component of the* iSuccess *model described in Chapter 5, advisors can interpret the results for clarity and perspective.*)
- Provide effective counseling services to individuals and groups. (*Professional advisors develop and conduct workshops delivered in one-on-one settings or group sessions that focus on deepening self-knowledge.*)
- Exercise institutional crisis intervention skills, and coordinate crisis intervention and response processes.
- Collaborate with other campus departments and organizations as well as surrounding community agencies and other institutions of higher education to address mental health concerns in a comprehensive, collaborative way. (*Collaboration provides the opportunity for integrative learning for both staff and students.*)
- Provide mental health consultation to faculty, staff, and campus behavioral assessment teams. (*Various professional advisors will have expertise in specific areas of interest such as the impact of nutrition on depression, or nutrition generally and how this contributes to physical and psychological well-being*).

Student Learning and Development

This competency "addresses the concepts and principles of student development and learning theory. This includes the ability to apply theory to improve and inform student affairs practice, as well as understanding teaching and training theory and practices" (ACPA and NASPA, 2010).

We highlight specific key competencies that relate directly to student success:

- Articulate theories and models that describe the development of college students and the conditions and practices that facilitate holistic development. (*Holistic refers to developing the whole person—intellect, well-being, and self-knowledge. The* iSuccess *model assists in facilitating holistic development.*)
- Identify and define types of theories (*e.g., learning, psychosocial and identity development, cognitive-structural, self-theory, strengths based*).
- Articulate one's own developmental journey and identify one's own informal theories of student development and learning (*often called "theories in use"*) and how they can be informed by formal theories to enhance work with students. (*Advisors and counselors draw upon lessons learned through life and their own therapy and participation in personal*

or professional development workshops to describe personal strengths and weaknesses.)
- Identify and take advantage of opportunities for curriculum and program development and construct, where appropriate, in order to encourage continual learning and developmental growth. (*Advisors and counselors seek out the future ideas that will shape their profession and gain perspectives and skills to better help students.*)
- Utilize theory to inform divisional and institutional policy and practice. (*The building block of the* iSuccess *model is scientific research into self-system and positive psychology attributions, therefore the* iSuccess *model will be helpful to the development of effective practices.*)
- Build and support inclusive and welcoming campus communities that promote deep learning and foster student success. (*Deep learning requires helping students to create personal meaning as a way to engage with academic material. Advisors and counselors initiate and sponsor student learning communities around mental health issues. One example is the student led "happiness clubs" at Stanford University.*)

Personal Foundations

This standard relates to those desired competencies of student affairs professionals, and what they should be able to do. (*We have extended this particular competency to include being able to impart these for students.*)

- Identify key elements of one's set of personal beliefs and commitments (*e.g., values, morals, goals, desires, self-definitions*), as well as the source of each (*e.g., self, peers, family, or one or more larger communities*).
- Identify one's primary work responsibilities and, with appropriate ongoing feedback, craft realistic summative self-appraisal of one's strengths and limitations.
- Describe the importance of one's professional and personal life to self, and recognize the intersection of each. (*If professionals gain experiential understanding of this process, they can better impart it to students.*)
- Articulate awareness and understanding of one's attitudes, values, beliefs, assumptions, biases, and identity as it impacts one's work with others, and take responsibility to develop personal cultural skills by participating in activities that challenge one's beliefs. (*Advisors can get outside the typical silo of their own work responsibilities and take on new beliefs about themselves and their work.*)

- Recognize and articulate healthy habits for better living. (*If you are the living embodiment of living the good life or of wellness, then celebrate and communicate what works!*)
- Articulate and understand that wellness is a broad concept composed of emotional, physical, social, environmental, relational, spiritual, and intellectual elements. (*This competency directly relates to the* iSuccess *model and its complete definition of wellness.*)
- Identify and describe personal and professional responsibilities inherent to excellence.
- Identify positive and negative impact on psychological wellness and, as appropriate, seek assistance from available resources.
- Recognize the importance of reflection in personal and professional development.
- Identify sources of dissonance and fulfillment in one's life and take appropriate steps in response.
- Recognize the relationship between one's professional and personal life, and develop plans to manage any related concerns.
- Analyze the impact one's health and wellness has on others, as well as their respective roles in creating mutual, positive relationships.
- Define excellence for one's self and evaluate how one's sense of excellence impacts self and others.
- Analyze personal experiences for potential deeper learning and growth, and engage with others in reflective discussions.
- Create and implement an individualized plan for healthy living.
- Demonstrate awareness of the psychological wellness of others in the workplace (university or college), and seek to engage with colleagues (students) in a way that supports such wellness (*If advisors have an approach or model that works, they should share it and celebrate it with others.*)
- Transfer thoughtful reflection into positive future action.

These professional competencies are all worthy and important. However, as we have seen in the previous chapter, examples of where and how these competencies are fully demonstrated through practice for institution-wide success are few and far between. This is most likely due to the lack of professional methods and practices in student affairs that are identified as foundational. Most student affairs academic programs that lead to professional degrees impart information about programs in higher education but do not teach methods on how to actually impart these competencies to help produce student success outcomes.

NACADA Student Success Standards

Academic advisors work to advance the educational development of students and help students make the most of their college experience. They include professional advisors, counselors, administrators, faculty, and other students. Some of the definitions of the work of academic advisors listed on the National Academic Advising Association (NACADA) website seem to overlap with those of student affairs professionals, where academic advisors give direction beyond academic matters to include social and personal development and help students match educational plans with life and career goals.

NACADA (2005) has a set of core values that guide the academic advising profession. According to this leading academic advising professional organization, advisors "foster individual potential" and "help students develop and reinforce realistic self-perceptions and help them use this information in mapping out their futures." Finally, in keeping with our new student success model, "advisors encourage self-reliance and support students as they strive to make informed and responsible decisions, set realistic goals, and develop lifelong learning and self-management skills."

All these core values reinforce the role of academic advising in student success and require an integrated, holistic view with a concomitant set of professional skills.

The following are the NACADA core values of academic advising that most directly relate to the student success model, with our comments in parenthesis and italic. These standards, used with permission by NACADA, are from its 2005 statement of core values of academic advising.

Core Value 1: Advisors Are Responsible to the Individuals They Advise

- Academic advising is an integral part of the educational process and affects students in numerous ways. As advisors enhance student learning and development, advisees have the opportunity to become participants in and contributors to their own education. In one of the most important potential outcomes of this process, academic advising fosters individual potential. (*The term "potential" in our student success model means a student's capacity for a good life filled with wellness. The responsibility of the advisor is to help students see and achieve their own unique potentials, meaning their unique purpose and dreams for their lives, not singularly fulfilling academic program requirements, as is too often the case.*)

- Advisors gain meaningful insights into students' diverse academic, social, and personal experiences and needs. (*In order to "gain insights," advisors need the* iSuccess *model with which to frame these holistic student needs.*)
- Advisors help students develop and reinforce realistic self-perceptions and help them use this information in mapping out their futures. (*In order to reinforce self-perceptions, advisors need a way of organizing numerous self-attributes, to reify or reflect back students' strengths and weaknesses. Mapping out futures requires inquiring into hopes and dreams, personally and professionally.*)
- Advisors encourage self-reliance and support students as they strive to make informed and responsible decisions, set realistic goals, and develop lifelong learning and self-management skills.
- Advisors respect students' rights to their individual beliefs and opinions. (*Advisors need to help students understand that they have their own set of beliefs and opinions that may be different from parents and peers.*)
- Advisors guide and teach students to understand and apply classroom concepts to everyday life. (*Advisors need to teach students how to reference concepts and experiences to self as a way to increase the transfer of knowledge among numerous domains.*)
- Advisors help students establish realistic goals and objectives and encourage them to be responsible for their own progress and success. (*Students need methods to be able to know where they are going, and to have milestones along the way. The* iSuccess *model, as expanded in the next chapter, provides advisors and students with an understanding of the journey, and how to know if they are on target or not. Additionally, individualized or personalized learning plans provide a map for advisors, faculty, and mentors to check in and see progress.*)

Core Value 2: Advisors Are Responsible for Involving Others, When Appropriate, in the Advising Process

- Academic advisors must develop relationships with personnel critical to student success including those in such diverse areas as admissions, orientation, instruction, financial aid, housing, health services, athletics, academic departments, and the registrar's office. They also must establish relationships with those who can attend to specific physical and educational needs of students, such as personnel in disability services, tutoring, psychological counseling, international study, and career development. (*The* iSuccess *model integrates departments and functions to help advisors communicate student needs and progress as learning outcomes. When multiple relationships have a common language or model to convey student self-knowledge, this facilitates positive coaching and problem solving.)*

Core Value 3: Advisors Are Responsible to Their Institutions
- Advisors encourage the use of models for the optimal delivery of academic advising programs within their institutions. (*Professional advisors should be seeking new models to maximize their effectiveness, increase their ability to empower student success, and meet their holistic needs.*)

Core Value 4: Advisors Are Responsible to Higher Education in General
- Advisors base their work with students on the most relevant theoretical perspectives and practices drawn from the fields of social sciences, the humanities, and education. (*The* iSuccess *model, with its high-impact practices, meets this professional standard because it is based on research.*)

The NACADA core values of advising have been produced "for the good of the profession." They indeed represent excellence in student success advising. However, it is also clear that the profession needs a set of practices and methods and common approaches that deliver results and empower the new direction of student success. In many ways, academic advisors are well suited to provide the broad base of whole-person counseling and education services needed by students in the new student success model. In our experience, academic advisors typically have interest and skills in numerous wellness dimensions. Additionally, they are typically highly educated and have the interpersonal skills needed by an effective life coach. They pride themselves on having a diverse set of worldly experiences that can and do inform their ability to guide young adults along a path of self-discovery.

However, they are too often professionally constrained by faculty or academic policies that require a focus mostly on curriculum and academics and do not provide cross-functional methods to develop the whole person.

CAS Student Success Standards

The Council for the Advancement of Standards (CAS) promotes standards in "student affairs, student services, and student development programs" (2015). CAS in higher education supports standards relevant to our student success model for counseling services and student learning in numerous domains and dimensions. The *iSuccess* model requires the integration of the numerous student success functions, and CAS holds that perspective as well. CAS sees student development integrated with academic learning. Recall that our formula for student success is the combination of intellectual growth plus student development, which is composed of self-knowledge and well-being. CAS believes counseling services should be integrated into the curricula and co-curricular life of the institution.

To achieve their mission, counseling services (CS) must contribute to

- Students' formal education, which includes both the curriculum and the co-curriculum
- Student progression and timely completion of educational goals
- Preparation of students for their careers, citizenship, and lives
- Student learning and development

The following student learning domains and dimensions have been used with permission by the CAS, from their 2015 *CAS Professional Standards for Higher Education* (9th ed.).

Student Learning and Development Domains and Dimensions

Domain: Knowledge acquisition, integration, construction, and application
- Dimensions: Understanding knowledge from a range of disciplines; connecting knowledge to other knowledge, ideas, and experiences; constructing knowledge; and relating knowledge to daily life

Domain: Cognitive complexity
- Dimensions: Critical thinking, reflective thinking, effective reasoning, and creativity

Domain: Intrapersonal development
- Dimensions: Realistic self-appraisal, self-understanding, and self-respect; identity development; commitment to ethics and integrity; and spiritual awareness

CS must be
- Intentionally designed
- Guided by theories and knowledge of learning and development
- Integrated into the life of the institution (*This is of particular note in that colleges and universities are having difficulty achieving this standard.*)
- Reflective of developmental and demographic profiles of the student population

- Responsive to needs of individuals, populations with distinct needs, and relevant constituencies
- Delivered using multiple formats, strategies, and contexts
- Designed to provide universal access

CS must collaborate with colleagues and departments across the institution to promote student learning and development, persistence, and success. (*Here is a good example of where CS has the charge to contribute their in-depth knowledge of the inner self of students to other university functions in order to produce whole-student wellness and student success outcomes.*)

To fulfill its mission, CS must provide the following services directly, through referral, or in collaboration:

- Individual counseling in areas of personal, educational, career development, interpersonal relationships, family, social, and psychological issues
- Group interventions (e.g., counseling, psychotherapy, support) to help students establish satisfying personal relationships and to become more effective in areas such as interpersonal processes, communication skills, decision making concerning personal relationships and educational or career matters, and the establishment of personal values
- Psychological testing and other assessment techniques to foster client self-understanding and decision-making

The CAS in higher education focuses on an integrated view of university support functions that produce self-understanding and self-knowledge outcomes from counseling and academic programming. They also see student success from a wellness perspective where students develop a wide array of competencies during their college learning careers that will last a lifetime.

IACS Student Success Standards

Counseling and psychological services professionals are dedicated to students' mental health. The International Association of Counseling Services (IACS) provides standards to counseling and psychological services (CAPS) departments, with specific standards that address our student success model.

The following standards have been used with permission by the IACS, from their 2014 *Standards for University and College Counseling Services*.

Student Success and Professional Standards

Counseling Services Roles and Functions

- The counseling service should play four essential roles in serving the university and college community: (1) provide counseling to students experiencing personal adjustment, vocational, developmental and/or psychological problems that require professional attention; (2) play a preventive role assisting students in identifying and learning skills which will assist them to effectively meet their educational and life goals; (3) support and enhance the healthy growth and development of students through consultation and outreach to the campus community; and (4) play a role in contributing to campus safety.

Individual and Group Counseling

- Counseling services must provide counseling interventions that are responsive to the diverse population of students experiencing ongoing or situational psychological or behavioral difficulties. (*In our view, group counseling is similar to classroom teaching and learning. Therefore, faculty teaching in their classrooms, student affairs first-year program coordinators teaching transition seminars, and career counselors teaching internship selection workshops, can all impart self-knowledge attributions if done so intentionally.*)

These direct service activities include the following criteria:

- Individual counseling must be provided and group counseling should be provided, which may include such issues as educational, career, personal, developmental, and relationship concerns. Services should be sufficient to meet the needs of students in a timely manner.
- Psychological tests and other diagnostic procedures should be used to make appropriate assessments of student functioning and treatment/disposition recommendations, to foster client self-understanding and decision making, and to determine the most effective intervention strategies possible within the limits of available resources.

IACS standards call for an integrated, holistic view of students with "educational, career, personal, developmental, and relationship" issues and concerns. In a group setting or one-on-one either in person or online, CAPS can extend resources to meet more diverse and growing needs for "client self-understanding and decision making." CAPS can become a center for wellness by offering workshops that address the holistic needs of today's students.

We highlight that CAPS should provide direct services that address educational, career, personal, and developmental issues. Further, they should play a preventative role in helping students meet their own educational and life goals, thereby once again asking students to define their own success. Counselors quite frankly do not know how to create this relationship, to shift the responsibility for self-determination and self-authorship for wellness to the student. Counseling professionals do not have the tools, counseling techniques, or coaching methods and models to assist them when encouraging students to define success for themselves.

As higher education institutions are using the predominant medical model for designing counseling and psychological services, prevention too often means administering diagnostic or assessments as prescreening methods. This is not prevention in our view. Prevention means embedding self-knowledge into those university functions most responsible for impacting students' mind-sets, for transforming their experiences. This entails embedding practices from the *iSuccess* model, thereby anticipating that people require a set of tools to heal adverse childhood experiences and other trauma while creating a new self and future.

In our research and work, we have found that CAPS can utilize the *iSuccess* high-impact practices in education programming that can actually prevent the symptoms referenced above when students experience personal adjustment, developmental, and/or psychological problems.

We want to underscore the importance of playing a preventative role in assisting students in identifying and developing learning skills to effectively meet their educational and life goals.

Using high-impact practices to teach students what healthy growth is contributes to campus safety through enhanced self-knowledge, with concomitant reduction in aggressive sexual behaviors, as one example. In another example, teaching self-knowledge contributes to campus safety by reducing drug and alcohol–related incidences requiring campus or community police responses.

NCDA Student Success Standards

Career development professionals help people achieve their career and life goals. The leading career development professional association, the National Career Development Association (NCDA), offers these standards or guidelines for career management/counseling that resonate with our student success model:

The following domains have been used with permission by the NCDA, from their 2007 *National Career Development Guidelines (NCDG) Framework.*

Personal Social Development Domain

- Goal PS1: Develop understanding of self to build and maintain a positive self-concept. (*Career management requires lifelong psychological and behavioral processes as well as awareness of the contextual influences shaping one's career over the life-span. Career development involves the person's creation of a career pattern, decision-making style, and the integration of life roles, values expression, and self-concepts. This requires a model through which the student and the career advisor may better understand what integration and self-concept reference and entail.*)
- Goal PS2: Develop positive interpersonal skills, including respect for diversity. (*Interpersonal understanding also includes knowledge of different types of learning styles, such as the Theory of Multiple Intelligences [MI]. Interpersonal skills are learned through internships, service learning, and leadership opportunities in a student's learning career.*)
- Goal PS3: Integrate growth and change into your career development. (*In the* iSelf *model dynamic change is understood by noticing the influence that a change in one attribute has on others. Therefore, personal change and growth occur hand in hand with professional or occupational pursuits that best fit these changes.*)
- Goal PS4: Balance personal, leisure, community, learner, family, and work roles.

Educational Achievement and Lifelong Learning Domain

- Goal ED1: Attain educational achievement and performance levels needed to reach your personal and career goals. (*"Personal" and "career" goals are interconnected, and as these occur almost simultaneously, they cannot be separated. Yet too often they are separated organizationally and functionally in higher education today, making it difficult for counseling professionals to be highly effective when impacting a student's future.*)
- Goal ED2: Participate in ongoing, lifelong learning experiences to enhance your ability to function effectively in a diverse and changing economy.

As students learn how to succeed in college and in life, they are striving for a vision of wellness that connects the domains of career with personal development. NCDA professionals have built into their competencies these distinctions and see them as integrated, not separate. We believe this calls for better integration of career counseling with personal counseling, as the two cannot and should not be separated.

NACE Student Success Standards

The Professional Standards for College and University Career Services written by the National Association of Colleges and Employers (NACE) establishes clear expectations for self-assessment and self-regulation, along with internal motivation and direction (2013; used with permission).

The use of professional standards in career services is intended to facilitate excellence in the creation, maintenance, and delivery of programs and services. Professionally derived standards, representing the perspectives of diverse practitioners and promulgated under the aegis of a professional association, provide an exceptional opportunity for practitioners to engage in processes of self-assessment and self-regulation that are internally motivated and self-directed.

Specifically, career services should help students and other designated clients to

- Promote self-assessment and self-regulation initiatives using professional standards as key factors in fostering improvement in programs, services, and processes.
- Develop self-knowledge related to career choice and work performance by identifying, assessing, and understanding their competencies, interests, values, and personal characteristics.
- Obtain educational and occupational information to aid their career and educational planning and to develop their understanding of the world of work.
- Select personally suitable academic programs and experiential opportunities that optimize future educational and employment options.

Proactive career services departments can be the primary source for delivering student self attributions that will sustain students throughout their life course, which will most likely include making numerous career changes. Of particular interest is the perspective that career services professionals take an integrated approach to help college students succeed ("select personally suitable academic programs and experiential opportunities"), combining self-knowledge with academic pursuits and student engagement.

AAC&U Essential Learning Outcomes

According to the Association of American Colleges and Universities (AAC&U), faculty are encouraged to design their courses to produce a set of outcomes as exemplars of professional excellence. Accreditors such as CAEP (Council for the Accreditation of Educator Preparation) and CACREP (Council for Accreditation of Counseling and Related Education Programs), among others, require additional metrics that are not included here. These standards are professionally specialized by academic program, whereas the AAC&U learning outcomes cross all academic programs. However, using our *iSuccess* high-impact practices will facilitate the production of both professionally specific and general academic programming outcomes.

To help guide faculty, the AAC&U (2002) offers a set of "essential learning outcomes" that assist not only faculty but those higher education units that are aligned for collective impact, such as student engagement, service learning, career internships, and leadership opportunities, among others.

The following essential learning outcomes have been used with permission by the AAC&U, from their 2002 *A New Vision for Learning*.

Knowledge of Human Cultures and the Physical and Natural World
- Through study in the sciences and mathematics, social sciences, humanities, histories, languages, and the arts. Focused by engagement with big questions, both contemporary and enduring.

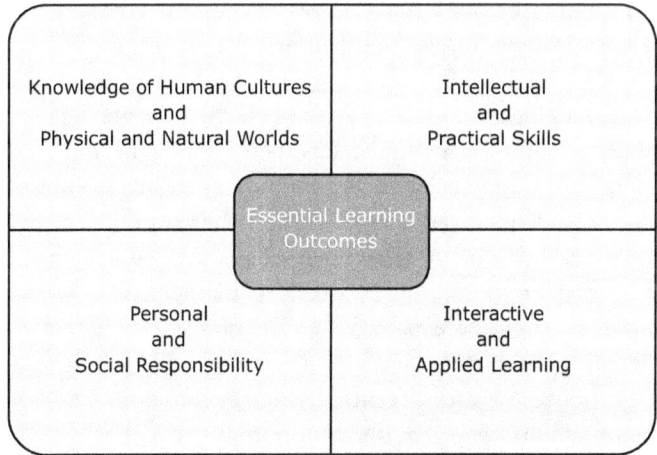

Figure 2. AAC&U Essential Learning Outcomes Diagram

Intellectual and Practical Skills

- Including inquiry and analysis, critical and creative thinking, written and oral communication, quantitative literacy, information literacy, teamwork and problem solving. Practiced extensively, across the curriculum, in the context of progressively more challenging problems, projects, and standards for performance.

Personal and Social Responsibility

- Including civic knowledge and engagement—local and global, intercultural knowledge and competence, ethical reasoning and action, foundations and skills for lifelong learning. Anchored through active involvement with diverse communities and real-world challenges.

Integrative and Applied Learning

- Including synthesis and advanced accomplishment across general and specialized studies. Demonstrated through the application of knowledge, skills, and responsibilities to new settings and complex problems.

To develop these qualities, education should foster

- Intellectual honesty
- Responsibility for society's moral health and social justice
- Active participation as a citizen of a diverse democracy
- Discernment of the ethical consequences of decisions and actions, deep understanding of one's self, and respect for the complex identities of others, their histories, and their cultures

AAC&U sees higher education's role in creating the greater good. Learning outcomes pertain to "deep understanding of one's self" and "personal and social responsibility," in which the responsible learner takes center stage, as is the case in our student success model. Further, the greater good that students are striving for and of which higher education is the trustee depends on citizens' sense of social responsibility and ethical judgment.

However, as would be expected, the organization's standards or recommended learning outcomes appear to favor cognitive strengths in critical thinking, synthesis, and discernment.

We must emphasize again that the *iSuccess* model is a breakthrough because it gives equal weight to noncognitive factors such as self-knowledge, motivation, emotional intelligence, and positive attitude, among others, and puts well-being at the center of the educator's mission.

All of the cognitive strengths will emerge if the student builds upon well-being and self-knowledge. Further, the *iSuccess* model has refined distinctions about personal responsibility that develop self-authorship and the ability to contribute to others—toward the greater good.

Final Thoughts

The reader may have noticed that the standards in this chapter require significant skills. How can one counselor or advisor work with approximately three hundred student clients and be able to impact them to these high standards? We need the *iSuccess* high-impact student success practices to change the culture of higher education.

This requires a shift to more of a team approach, a culture where all front-line educators are aligned and on board with a singular focus upon well-being and self-knowledge as the core of student success. To do this requires expertise, time, and training on this integrated perspective.

Leading professional organizations such as ACPA, NASPA, NACADA, CAS, NCDA, NACE, IACS, and AAC&U will collectively benefit from an integrated model and set of high-impact practices to empower student success. In the next chapter, we present the first integrated, research-based set of student success professional practices to help practitioners produce results consistent with their fields' competencies.

CHAPTER 5

STUDENT SUCCESS HIGH-IMPACT PRACTICES

The *iSuccess* model provides an integrated and interdisciplinary approach to support student success. As we have described previously, self-knowledge and well-being are at the heart of student success—especially from the student's point of view.

In previous chapters we have built the case that higher education is changing, and so too are missions of a select few visionary institutions. The professional associations are already placing high value on integrated approaches and personal and self-knowledge attributions. We then argued that even though the professions have indeed developed standards and competencies that deal directly with student success, they need a set of practices that work effectively in and across all five student success functions.

We further discussed George Kuh's high-impact *educational* practices and six key elements, demonstrating that even though these are accepted high-impact practices, they do not go far enough in developing the whole person, nor do they provide the methods and tools to produce well-being results. Even more to the point, they do not provide students with what they need to create their own pathways to success and a positive life course trajectories, complete with a vision for an extraordinary quality of life filled with wellness. Our *iSuccess* model, with three high-impact *student success* practices, teaches students how to transform their lives. (From this point forward, the "high-impact" designation will refer only to the three high-impact practices in the *iSuccess* model.)

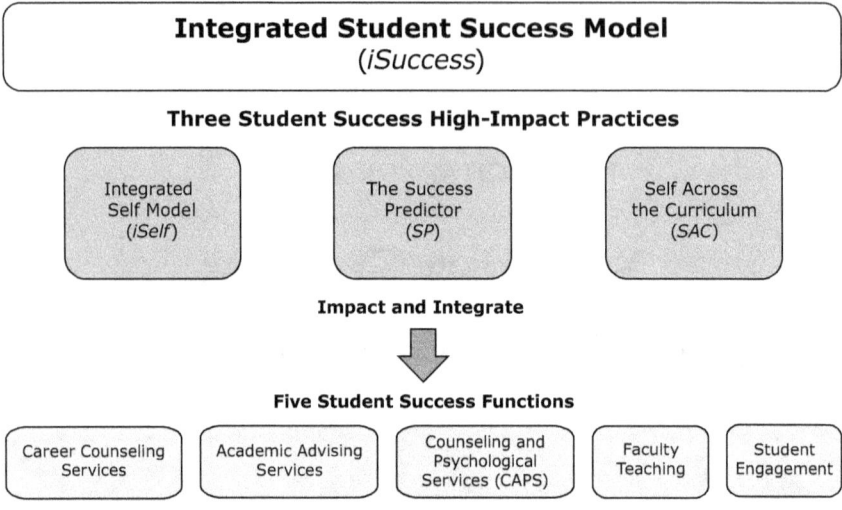

Figure 3. *Integrated Student Success* Model (*iSuccess*)

The *iSuccess* model includes three, research-based student success high-impact practices for imparting self-knowledge to students throughout the college experience. These practices give student success professionals the tools they need to be effective when working with students in their respective fields, and to integrate their efforts with other university student success functions:

- The *Integrated Self* (known as *iSelf*) is a model for understanding the multiple dimensions of self-knowledge, or the whole person.
- *Self Across the Curriculum* (*SAC*) is a pedagogy for implementing the *Integrated Self* (*iSelf*) model.
- The *Success Predictor* (*SP*) is an assessment and intervention instrument, used as a preventative approach to well-being and student success.

Combined, these three high-impact practices empower students to create an extraordinary life, filled with an understanding of unique potential, life purpose, and dreams. When students understand *iSelf* attributes, they are on the path to self-knowledge, wellness, and student success.

Figure 3 depicts the relationship dynamics in the *iSuccess* model.

Student Transformation

Our expertise is student transformation, helping students and those who support them transform the quality of their lives to ones filled with well-being or wellness. A *transformed mind-set* (or simply *transformation*) is a deep change at a being level within a human being. It is a fundamental, systemic change in the conscious awareness of self and others. It is a change in one's consciousness—the understanding of numerous self-components and freedom to be who one really is, not who one "should" be or is expected to be. It impacts mind, body, and soul dimensions. It is usually characterized by having achieved a state of self-actualization, a new understanding that includes examining and changing deeply held, unconscious beliefs and knowing one's purpose in life as a higher calling in life to give back to others. A student with a transformed mind-set has experienced all (or most) of the *iSelf* model's multiple dimensions of self-knowledge. An *untransformed mind-set* is the opposite—one has no motivation to achieve self-actualization, no motivation to examine or change beliefs, and no interest in discovering a higher calling in life, and one does not have an interest in learning about the self or any self-attributions common to all yet unique to each.

Students experience a shift in their perspectives about who they are and the future difference they are called to make and can dream about making. This is why the *iSelf* model, *Self Across the Curriculum*, and the *Success Predictor* all represent effective, high-impact practices for use by college academic advising departments, first-year experience programs, campus alcohol and drug awareness programs, relationships programs, and career advising, among numerous student success activities. They draw upon an integrated model of self with positive psychology distinctions that connect with college-aged adolescents and young adults, and they utilize strengths-based counseling to empower students to create their own paths toward academic, career, and life success.

Using Self-Knowledge to Make a Difference

In the current information age, actionable knowledge is the central resource to create the wealth that is traditionally seen as the pathway to a better society and better life. Forces are shaping the existing paradigm in which to redefine the good life. In this age, a better society will be based on the creation of personal meaning for each individual through the use of knowledge and information. Knowledge is used to make a difference in society. Each individual will take the knowledge available and create new knowledge and new services to make things better in terms of quality of life, happiness, and well-being.

The three high-impact student success practices make it possible to take knowledge and channel it toward personal purpose and making a unique contribution to the world. We would argue that implementing these high-impact practices through the complete college experience will serve to make self-knowledge actionable, toward a greater good, not toward merely acquiring wealth or a professional pursuit.

Using one of the three high-impact practices, the *iSelf* model, as one's lens, the individual self uses and creates knowledge with the intent of building a better life—not always for economic value but for community value and for psychological and physical well-being. The three high-impact student success practices are the building blocks of student transformation. Students need rich distinctions to better understand themselves precisely because people are so complex. And when placed in modern 21st-century society, characterized by a fast pace of change, in-depth understanding of self acts as a compass and map toward lifelong learning and success.

As counselors, teachers, and higher education leaders, we have applied the ideas presented here in this book, with transformational results in terms of the quality of people's lives and their psychological and physical well-being. We believe that the idea of teaching self-knowledge to all through higher education to improve mental and physical well-being represents a breakthrough in what it means to be human, with all the inherent possibilities for a better life, for everyone. In short, focusing on the self in higher education is an idea whose time has come.

What is transformative about our work and the three high-impact student success practices is that we demonstrate through research and practice that students have a higher purpose that is driving their thoughts, feelings, and actions, a DNA of consciousness that, when learned, transforms their quality of life.

We have researched student's needs for more than thirty years and have documented these changing developmental needs through our books, conference presentations, and articles. Most notably, however, we have developed research-based, evidence-based programs that actually teach adolescents and young adults how to determine their own vision of success, metrics for measuring, and pathways to achieve.

How do we inspire students to pursue a college education and then complete it once enrolled? A high-impact practice that we have used at the college level is to teach students how to refer, or apply, what they are learning to themselves. Additionally, in his classes as a professor, and as dean of a school of education, coauthor Henry used the *iSelf* model, the *Self Across the Curriculum* (*SAC*), and the *Success Predictor* (*SP*) instrument to inspire students to do whatever it takes to finish their degree. Once students are able to personally formulate their own purpose and dreams for their lives, they are committed, inspired, and motivated to overcome the numerous obstacles to a pathway of success. Henry has seen students obtain the monetary resources required to finance their education—the most often cited source of frustration causing students to drop out. He has helped students use the *Success Predictor* to overcome anxiety and or depression during college years and develop a stronger psychological state of mind.

The Importance of Self-Knowledge

As discussed earlier, self-knowledge is the number one protector factor for schools and parents to impart. We know that college students today are feeling many stresses associated with modern life. Research has shown that these stressors lead to drug and alcohol use, depression, obesity and other eating disorders, suicide, bullying, and cutting, among others. Students need new strategies to deal with these concerns as they go through them and for the rest of their lives. When we help our students handle these everyday stressors and manifestations by teaching self-knowledge as the focus of student success, they are intrinsically motivated to learn and, in our experience, perform way beyond our highest expectations.

It is critical for educators to shift their focus to imparting self-system and positive psychology attributes in order to teach college students how to flourish in life through curricula and co-curricular programming. Until now, there has been no unifying model of self or what constitutes the whole person in student success practices that can be used for both assessments and interventions. If we utilize a common model of self, then we can have better results across professional services in teaching and learning, counseling and psychological services (CAPS), academic advising, student engagement, and career counseling. If we want to see both academic and well-being outcomes from student success processes, then we need to utilize the *iSelf* model. As a process, learning that occurs in the classroom and career and personal counseling sessions is the same. The learning pathway is the self and one or more components of the *iSelf* model.

Student success professionals can use the *iSelf* model as a unifying framework, a working model of how to utilize positive psychology and an integrative psychology approach in higher education across all student success functions. Our student success model places the holistic needs of students at the center, and therefore the *iSelf* model is a high-impact practice.

Using the *iSelf* model, faculty, academic advisors, career counselors, CAPS professionals, and student engagement educators have access to a view of the whole person. A whole person has a brain, a mind, a body, and a soul. We all have emotions and varying cognitive capabilities, and all these make up the self of an individual. Most important, these component parts of the whole person are not separate, but integrated. Too often researchers and academics isolate one or two of these attributes in an attempt to study them; this may make sense from a pure research perspective, but it does not make any sense to advancing our understanding and transformation of human beings. We are not that simple. Teachers, advisors, and counselors need to acknowledge, serve, and operate across the integrated self of students, and not single out one or two attributes to observe and develop.

So too when discussing a student-centered approach to student success, we need to take an integrated, institutional perspective of all five of the student success functions. When we do this, we shape a framework of a single model of higher education student success, along with a single model of how to understand and empower our students.

Emotions and Cognition

Dr. Frederick Brown, a leading psychology of well-being researcher and professor at The Pennsylvania State University, affirms the importance of the *iSelf* model in education and provides a clear summary:

> Dr. Brzycki's novel concept of the *iSelf* uses 21st-century terminology for terms earlier introduced to convey less comprehensive concepts such as soul, reality-oriented ego, and mind. However, his *iSelf* emerges from the interaction of current scientific information about the direct influence by emotions, both positive and negative, upon cognitive functioning. These emotions, in turn, are based upon personal relevancy and meaningfulness and are the controlling switch by which effective learning takes place or not. A positive emotional approach facilitates a sense of well-being that, in turn, enhances a willingness to learn. The outcome, in turn, promotes a greater sense of well-being and less reason for persons to engage in self-destructive behaviors. These senseless acts include addictions, cutting, vandalism, and the current developing insensitivity to others, shown by increasing acts of juvenile cruelty and brutality face-to-face and through electronic social media.

Note the critical interaction or dynamic between emotions, cognition, and well-being, a holistic view of the inside of the mind of the student in a higher education learning experience. Student success programming and methods require the inclusion of this dynamic to improve whole-person outcomes.

When we use the high-impact student success methods, we help students engage in learning experiences that harness the motivations and emotional need to learn, creating more direct pathways to deeper learning that transfer across multiple domains in life. When we view students through the *iSelf* lens, we can teach self-knowledge so that natural internal self-motivations are engaged toward personal dreams and the manifestation of life's purpose. In both teaching and student affairs counseling settings, the student works in partnership with the teacher or counselor to create those learning activities (such as projects, internships, or service learning) that best suit and change the brain functioning to meet the mind's purpose and dreams and the emotional responses to these.

The *iSelf* model helps effective teachers teach students important self-distinctions using subject content in their classrooms. What then occurs is a more direct transfer of knowledge. The self is the context that makes the academic content meaningful and therefore creates a deeper understanding.

Emotional intelligence is important to develop through college experiences, as emotions tell each of us what is important to learn, know, and be able to do. Our higher education institutions have largely ignored this critical dimension of the self and of learning. This is tragic because faculty are searching for ways to not only engage their students in learning academic content but also make learning more meaningful and purposeful for each student. We need to impart emotional intelligence, self-awareness, and health through student success processes so that we can create a more thoughtful and civil society with honest debate about how to solve the real and deep problems we confront.

The self, and in particular the *Integrated Self* or *iSelf* model, is a lens through which to view and understand the condition of human being and the reality we have created. This model focuses on ways in which education helps people reach their full and unique potentials in life. The *iSelf* model is situated at the intersection of psychology and education, and it challenges scholars and practitioners alike to forge new views and methods that will improve the quality of our lives.

Integrated Self Model (*iSelf*)

The self is socially constructed through a dynamic interaction between inter-psychological and intrapsychological processes.

The *iSelf* is a model for understanding the multiple dimensions of the self, and for building an integrated self. We developed the model through research in psychology and education in order to improve academic and well-being outcomes (Brzycki, 2009; 2010). The *iSelf* model also draws upon our numerous clinical experiences where the model of self, the theoretical applications, and actual transformations support the ideas presented and discussed.

The *Integrated Self* (*iSelf*) model incorporates self-system and positive psychology attributes that reinforce one another through development across the life-span and through K-16 formal schooling experiences. An analogy would be a mobile, where one element, when moved, impacts all other component parts to varying degrees.

By way of example, if a student is clear about her unique purpose in life (one attribute), this may impact her motivation to succeed (another attribute) by making larger contributions to the greater good envisioned. Previous research conducted on self-system and positive psychology attributes typically isolates one of many attributes or at most looks at the relationship between only one attribute and school achievement. That view minimizes the holistic nature and dynamic that exists among all component parts of the self.

The *iSelf* model integrates component parts from self-system and positive psychology attributes. It is a paradigm for imparting self-knowledge through the five student success higher education functions in the *iSuccess* model.

The *iSelf* model can be used as a framework for frontline educators, higher education teaching faculty and administrators, students in college, university academic and first-year experience advisors, counseling and psychological services, and career counselors.

The *iSelf* model incorporates self-attributes identified by numerous progressive educators and humanistic psychologists. William James (1900) offered a view of a self in the early 1890s: "A man's self is the sum of all that he can call his" (p. 291). According to James, this includes the inner dimensions of self, such as feelings, thoughts, and spiritual understandings, and the outer dimensions of self, such as physical and social interactions. The inward life is the central nucleus of the self. John Dewey (1916) extended key distinctions of the self and their application to education to include moral development, interests, conscious purpose, desire, and reflection, among others. He also placed these distinctions at the center of teaching and learning, with what is known to educators as "child-centered pedagogy," which characterized the progressive movement throughout the 1920s and into the early 1950s (Cremin, 1964). Dewey (1916) encouraged educators to never see the self as complete—that it is always "becoming," which we take to mean always changing, growing, and developing.

The Whole Person

The *iSelf* model represents what is going on holistically inside a person. It is a way to conceptualize all the components of the self. When we discuss the self of a person, we speak in terms of attributes (and, interchangeably in this book, attributions). An attribute is a functioning mechanism of the self that includes an understanding of internal mind and what is represented externally as an expression. Each attribute influences the dynamic equilibrium of the whole self.

In Figure 4, we group the *iSelf* attributes in order to provide the reader with an entry point, but the organization and interplay of the attributes constantly changes. The mind, body, and soul enhance the attributes, and the attributes enhance the mind, body, and soul, in a dynamic relationship.

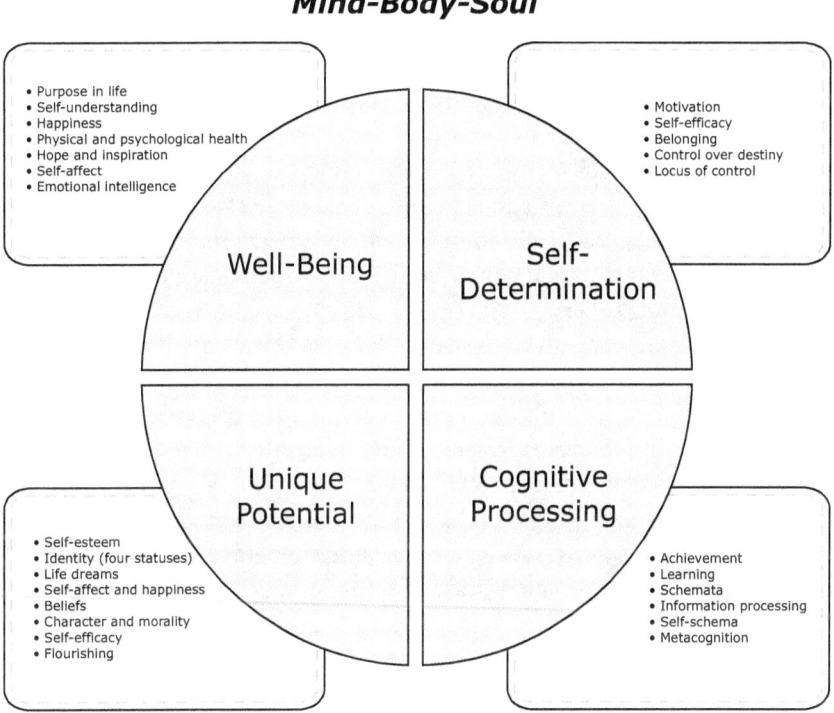

Figure 4. The *iSelf* Model: Component Parts That Include Self-System and Positive Psychology Attributes

Self-System Attributes Defined

Developmental psychologist Susan Harter offers an integrated construct of the self she calls the "self-system" (Harter, 1999). By "system" she does not mean to establish a predictable view of how component parts of the self operate.

Rather, Harter means to offer a holistic view that is consistent with that of Dewey (1900; 1902; 1916) and James (1900; 1992), where a self is the sum of all dynamic component parts.

Building upon Harter's (1999) concepts and conceptualization, we define the self-system and self-system attributes to consist of self-concept, self-esteem, self-efficacy, self-understanding, identity, locus of control, self-affects, and self-schemas.

Self-Concept

This refers to how you view yourself; your frame made up of important references.

Self-image and self-perception are synonymous terms. Important references can be your interests and activities. These interests are usually grouped or categorized (e.g., academic and nonacademic, peer group, intellectual and nonintellectual, physical and nonphysical, athletic and nonathletic, artistic and nonartistic, among others).

Self-concept most often develops through becoming aware of innate strengths and developing qualities and characteristics and the quality of the experience of performance when exercising these. It develops through a process of attempting to express an innate desire or interest combined with the messages received through the experience. An individual's innate cognitive strengths are commonly organized along the lines of Gardner's (1983) Theory of Multiple Intelligences (MI), which include strengths defined as interpersonal and intrapersonal, naturalistic and spiritual, logical and linguistic, kinesthetic and spatial, and musical and artistic.

Self-Esteem

This refers to the value that you place upon those strengths, characteristics, and activities that make up your self-concept—values such as feeling good or bad about your abilities in math, sports, or music. Numerous scholars and researchers have found a direct correlation between self-esteem and performance.

The following quote underscores the important connection between negative self-esteem and therefore negative self-system constructs and well-being outcomes: "a child who experiences attachment figures as rejecting or emotionally unavailable and non-supportive will construct a working model of the self as unlovable, incompetent, and generally unworthy" (Harter, 1999, p. 13). Thus "the most common affective correlate of negative self-perceptions is depression. In the extreme, depressive reactions associated with negative self-perceptions will lead to suicidal behaviors" (Harter and Marold, 1992, p. 13; Locker and Cropley, 2004).

Self-Efficacy

This refers to your beliefs about your potentialities and about your capacity to grow and learn to become the person you want to become. Efficacy is the belief that you can accomplish a goal. Albert Bandura (1997) and Paul Pintrich and Dale Schunk (2002) conceptualized four sources of self-efficacy that are relevant to our discussion:

The first source is mastery experiences, which are our direct experiences of success or failure. Successes raise our efficacy beliefs, and failures lower our efficacy beliefs. The second is physiological and emotional arousal, which impacts efficacy beliefs depending on whether we are anxious or worried (low efficacy) or excited or happy (high efficacy). The third is vicarious experience, which ties our efficacy beliefs to someone who models accomplishments and the degree to which we identify with the model. When the model performs well, our efficacy increases, but when the model performs poorly, our efficacy expectations decrease. The fourth, social persuasion, uses the power of performance feedback to boost efficacy expectations, but efficacy will only be enhanced if the persuader is credible, trustworthy, and an expert.

Self-efficacy is the leading antecedent to student aspirations and career trajectories (Bandura et al., 2001) and performance in the classroom (Pajares, 1996). Indeed, a strong self-system enables individuals to exercise a measure of control over their thoughts, feelings, and actions (Bandura, 1986).

Self-Understanding

This refers to the conscious knowing that you are a separate self from your circumstances, family, society, culture, media, and peers. It is the knowing that you have a separate way of feeling, experiencing events, and interpreting the world, and a personal understanding of your uniqueness vis-à-vis others.

Self-understanding is sometimes used synonymously with self-knowledge; however, this is a distinction with a difference. Self-knowledge is the sum or holistic view of one's self in all of its component parts. In our *iSelf* model, there are thirty component parts that make up self-knowledge. Self-understanding is one component part or attribute, important in that it allows us to be separate from others and from our circumstances or even past beliefs and assumptions.

This attribute is important in that often we do not have healthy boundaries between ourselves and others, or between ourselves and our control over substances such as unhealthy foods, drugs, and alcohol. Expressions of self-understanding include higher and higher levels of consciousness, awareness that there are higher states and that they contribute to enlightened views.

College-aged adolescents and young adults who possess self-understanding grow up to be more accomplished in the domain of school and later in life as healthier adults (Hawkins, et al, 2008).

Identity

This refers to your distinct personality. Erik Erikson (1963; 1968; 1980) posited that we form and reform our identities over the course of a lifetime and at different and distinct stages of development. His idea of developing and changing mental schemas inform the *iSelf* model: an increasing sense of identity is experienced preconsciously as a sense of psychosocial well-being. Its most obvious concomitants are feeling of being at home in one's body, a sense of "knowing where one is going," and an inner assuredness of anticipated recognition from those who count. Such a sense of identity, however, is never gained nor maintained once and for all. Like a "good conscience," it is constantly lost and regained (Erikson, 1980, p. 128).

Building on Erikson's work, James Marcia asserts that there are four identity statuses, depending on whether people have explored options and made commitments (Marcia, 1991; 1994; 2002). The first is identity achievement, which requires the exploration of both realistic and unrealistic options and commits to pursuing a choice or choices made. The second is identity foreclosure, which is a commitment made without exploration (no experimentation with a range of options) but simply commits based on the goals, values, and lifestyle of others. The third is identity diffusion, when individuals do not explore or commit, but rather reach no conclusions about who they are, what they want to do with their lives, or who they want to become as a person—no direction. Adolescents who experience diffusion may be apathetic and withdrawn, with little hope for the future, or they may be openly rebellious (Berger and Thompson, 1995; Kroger, 1996). The fourth is identity moratorium, when the individual is in the midst of struggling with choices, still exploring options, but delaying committing to personal and or professional growth or direction

(Woolfolk, 2004). In this fourth status, an individual is apt to suffer from an identity crisis, common among young adults in college or recently postcollege.

Locus of Control

This refers to your belief system regarding the causes of experiences and the factors to which you attribute success or failure (Rotter, 1966). There is a critical distinction between internal and external locus of control in assessing beliefs about who has influence over one's life course. A healthy internal locus of control suggests that an individual attributes success to her own efforts and abilities. A person who expects to succeed will be more internally motivated and more likely to want to learn, take full responsibility for the circumstances in her life, and know she can change them to manifest her own destiny in life.

External locus of control suggests that a person attributes success to luck or fate or to circumstances outside of one's self and control. People with external locus of control are more likely to experience anxiety, resignation, depression, and withdrawal from fully experiencing life—to be a victim of their circumstances.

Self-Schema

This refers to a mental model made up of bits of information that are representations of both your internal beliefs and external cultural beliefs known as schemata. The schema organizes the schemata, for example, into beliefs learned from life's experiences. The schema is where meaning is made or processed between one's internal and external worlds to create one's reality.

Our schemas are mental structures that influence our perception of reality, interpretation of experiences, and then how we plan and take action. A self-schema is one's personal paradigm of reality. The self-schema takes incoming information and uses it to create the additional self-attributes, such as self-concept, self-efficacy, identity, meaning, and affect/emotions; it is critical in making us uniquely who we are.

Personal as well as cultural beliefs make up an individual's paradigm of reality and how one sees oneself and one's world. Schema theory provides the critical link between the internal and external self and provides the space for the creation of mind. Cognitive sociologist and Princeton professor Paul DiMaggio (1997) focuses on "schema theory as especially relevant to the representation of social phenomena" (DiMaggio, 1997, p. 283) and "the ways in which social identities enter into the constitution of individual selves"

(DiMaggio, 1997, p. 275). Cultural beliefs are integrated into the self as schemata, which are acquired "by individuals during development" (DiMaggio, 1997, p. 280). Reflecting the social construction of the mind, and the inescapable influence of peer groups in schools, family, and the culture at large, Harvard University educational philosopher Israel Scheffler asserted, "development of self-knowledge grows out of the social process" (Scheffler, 1985, p. 25).

Self-Affect

This refers to a personal feeling or emotion that is sometimes difficult to use language to describe because it is an experience. It involves multiple sensations to varying degrees. "Without affect, feelings do not feel because they have no intensity, and without feelings, rational decision-making becomes problematic" (Damasio, 1994, p. 22). Also, "affect plays an important role in determining the relationship between our bodies, our environment, and others, and the subjective experience that we feel/think as affect dissolves into experience" (Shouse, 2005). In short, self-affect is the ability to feel and to know that you are feeling emotions.

Positive Psychology Attributes

The *iSelf* model also incorporates attributes from positive psychology. Positive psychology is an evolution of the cognitive developmental and humanistic views of the self. We define positive psychology attributes (Csikszentmihalyi, 1993; Seligman and Csikszentmihalyi, 2000; Snyder and Lopez, 2002) to consist of such commonly understood concepts as life purpose, life satisfaction, life meaning, happiness, intrinsic motivation, inspiration, and possible selves, where these contribute to psychological and subjective well-being outcomes (Ryan and Deci, 2001; Lent, Singley, Sheu, and Gainor, 2005) and therefore are important protective factors for educators, counselors, and health professionals to consider.

Positive psychology introduces more existential perspectives to embrace spirituality, happiness, hope, and dreams.

Past American Psychological Association president and professor Martin Seligman (2000; 2005; 2011) asserts that the goal of traditional psychology "was to bring patients from a negative, ailing state to a neutral normal state—from a minus five to a zero" (Seligman in Wallis, 2005). The vision of positive psychology is to bring human beings from zero to plus five and answer the question, "What are the enabling conditions that make human beings flourish" (Seligman, 2000)? This is an important question for faculty, counselors, and all higher education professionals to consider when empowering the full and unique potentials of all students, from all cultures and backgrounds.

The *iSelf* model incorporates these positive psychology attributes: life purpose and spirituality; life meaning; intrinsic motivation; happiness; inspiration, hope, and dreams; possible selves; self-determination; emotional intelligence and positive emotions; well-being; and creativity.

Life Purpose and Spirituality

This refers to the reason you are here, for your existence (raison d'être), and describes or includes your basic nature or being: the essence of a human being, the totality of all things that exist, the qualities that constitute existence or essence, and your basic nature. It includes your mission in life as an avenue or pathway to manifest your life's purpose—an inner calling to pursue an activity or perform a service, a vocation, the area of life where you will manifest your purpose. This calling is spiritual in nature and involves a connection with a higher power, an uplifting and transcending force, or feeling of need: to feel the calling to contribute to the human condition in some way, unique to you and your life experiences and views of a better world or greater good. It is what we commit our lives to, bigger than ourselves, using our unique talents, values, and vision in the service of creating a better world. It is part of the underlying motivation and driving force that guides our actions and brings us fulfillment. Our purpose is bigger than we are; it is a lifelong process that we can continuously discover, reflect and improve upon, and compels us to make a difference in our lives, the lives of others, and the condition of the world.

This George Bernard Shaw quote characterizes the spirit of a person's purpose:

> This is the true joy in life, the being used for a purpose recognized by yourself as a mighty one; the being a force of nature instead of a feverish selfish little clod of ailments and grievances complaining that the world will not devote itself to making you happy. I want to be thoroughly used up when I die, for the harder I work the more I live. I rejoice in life for its own sake. Life is no "brief candle" to me. It is a sort of splendid torch which I have got hold of for the moment, and I want to make it burn as brightly as possible before handing it on to future generations. (*Man and Superman*, 1973)

Life Meaning

Today's millennials and GenZ students are seeking meaningful experiences and a meaningful life. This involves being able to process the vast amounts of information that you take in constantly and then create meaning, a deeper understanding, connecting with the attributes of the self. This is the process of interpreting information as relevant to some aspect of yourself or your life, special to you and the way you interpret life events. Taking information and consciously placing meaning on it can be self-referential or other-referential.

Self-referential involves connecting or encoding with an internal self-attribute, where other-referential involves connecting with external context, such as relationships or renewable energy, usually categorized as "other" or "all."

Intrinsic Motivation

This is your inner drive to achieve to accomplish or reach a desired state. This inner drive may come from instinct, a deep subconscious desire, or a conscious want, and is usually juxtaposed with extrinsic motivation, which refers to the external forces that move you to act. Learning adds to and changes our internal motivations to manifest that which we desire for our best self-interest.

When you learn that you have a new belief about the importance of relationships and you define yourself by this belief, then you are internally motivated to develop meaningful relationships that reinforce your belief system. "Learners who are intrinsically motivated may engage in an activity because it gives them pleasure, helps them develop a skill they think is important, or is the ethically and morally right thing to do" (Ormrod, 2011).

Happiness

This is an emotion of elation, of joy, of feeling that all is well. An experience that is interpreted as a state of being happy, happiness is a conscious thought. The term subjective happiness is often used because there is no absolute state; it is an interpretation of an experience that makes you happy. So while feelings of elation can be temporarily created in our brain with mood-altering drugs, lasting happiness requires more proactive awareness and decision-making. It is often said that happiness is a choice.

The experience reflects a deeper want has been realized. This deeper want may be a conscious or intuitive desire. Satisfaction is an example of a feeling of happiness—evidence that a want or desire or intended result has been realized or manifest. Happiness occurs when the resulting circumstances in your life match your dreams, commitments, and goals for your life, after taking action or implementing a strategy to produce results. People thrive on having goals, and there are always more goals to set for the future; therefore happiness require finding a dynamic equilibrium between your wants and the evidence that these wants will be or have been achieved.

A person's awareness of wants and desires needs to come into balance with her perception of the evidence or circumstances that reflect the achievement of her desires. This awareness and perception are a creative act.

Inspiration, Hope, and Dreams

These all involve a vision of a future state, including all circumstances and emotions: what you can see that you want in your mind's eye. You are inspired to dream, to spark the insight or seed of a desired future state through inspiration either from another person or or within your inner consciousness or life experience; you hope that you can manifest that dream. It is what you see in the future, like a dream of what is possible, and a mental image produced by the imagination to see in your mind's eye, unusual competence or perception, and intelligent foresight. "Hopeful thought reflects the belief that one can find pathways to desired goals [and envisioned dreams] and then become motivated to use those pathways" (Snyder, Rand, and Sigmon, 2005, p. 257).

To relate the importance of instilling hope in students and their visions of their own success that includes its effect on wellness, Lopez (2009) provided the following definition:

> Hopeful students see the future as better than the present, and believe they have the power to make it so. These students are energetic and full of life. They are able to develop many strategies to reach goals and plan contingencies in the event that they are faced with problems along the way. As such, obstacles are viewed as challenges to overcome and are bypassed by garnering support and/or implementing alternative pathways. Perceiving the likelihood of good outcomes, these students focus on success and, therefore, experience greater positive affect and less distress. Generally, high-hope people experience less anxiety and less stress specific to test-taking situations. (p. 1)

Possible Selves

This is a conception that you can become what you see is possible. It is a thought process where you reflect upon and inquire into "what if" questions and possible scenarios for who you can become and your life direction. You believe either that you are locked into a single way of being or becoming or that you can exercise freedom to change who you are and your life. The possible selves attribute represents your ideas of what you might become, what you would like to become, and what you are afraid of becoming, and thus provide a conceptual link between cognition and motivation. Possible selves include the cognitive components of hopes, fears, goals, and threats; they give the specific self-relevant form, meaning, organization, and direction to these dynamics. It is suggested that possible selves function as incentives for future behavior and provide an evaluative and interpretive context for the current view of self (Markus and Nurious, 1986, p. 1).

Self-Determination

Self-determination is defined by three needs: the need to control the course of your life (autonomy), the need to be effective in dealing with your environment (competence), and the need to have close, affectionate relationships (relatedness). "To be self-determined is to endorse one's actions at the highest level of reflection [and] when self-determined people experience a sense of freedom to do what is interesting, personally important, and revitalizing" (Deci and Ryan, 1985).

Emotional Intelligence and Positive Emotions

This is your ability to discern numerous subtle distinctions of a wide range of emotions, such as sadness and depression, happiness and elation, anger and rage. This involves the ability to manage the emotions with thought and to express them effectively and appropriately within a context. To recognize emotions in others is a quality of empathy or the ability to empathize.

According to Goleman (1995), emotional intelligence consists of the capacity for each or all of these ingredients: confidence, curiosity, intentionality, self-control, relatedness, capacity to communicate, and cooperativeness (p. 194). Positive emotions consist of episodes of pleasure, happiness, energy, confidence, positive mood, enthusiasm, love and caring, and so on.

Well-Being

This refers to your psychological and physical health, where health is not simply the absence of illness, as in mental illness, but the more positive connotation of how well your life is going; your well-being is what is good for you.

Well-being includes emotional health, vitality and satisfaction, life direction and ability to make a difference, physical health and energy to function fully, healthy behaviors such as diet and exercise, quality of relationships, financial stability, experiencing a high quality of life, and living a good life. We refer throughout this book to well-being as the core of student success and as an imperative to a positive life trajectory. So while we include well-being here as a positive psychology attribute, we have been using it to describe the desired result of self-knowledge and the purpose of higher education. The greater good includes the well-being of all people.

Creativity

This involves making connections between ideas or experiences that were previously unconnected (Robinson, 2001, p. 11). Creative people are those who express unusual thoughts, who are interesting and stimulating—people who appear to be unusually bright. They are people who experience the world in novel and original ways, people whose perceptions are fresh, whose judgments are insightful, who may make important discoveries that only they can envision. These individuals often change our culture in some important way (e.g., Da Vinci, Edison, Picasso, Einstein; Csikszentmihalyi, 1996, pp. 25–26). Everyone has the capacity for creativity. Being creative involves coming up with something new—for example, a new idea out of nothing that is worthwhile and useful and a unique expression of you.

In 1998 the annual report of the American Psychological Association introduced this newest branch of psychology, called positive psychology, whose concepts include happiness, well-being, purpose in life, and emotional intelligence, among other distinctly human and humanistic traits. This insight offers educators multiple pathways to develop the personalized human goodness that lies within each of us, regardless of race, socioeconomic background, intellectual DNA, emotional and psychological capabilities, or gender.

iSelf Implementation

The *iSelf* model forms the foundation for student success; it enhances and strengthens the five student success model functions by providing professionals with enlightening self-system and positive psychology concepts and attributions such as happiness, purpose in life, and well-being. Further, it provides advisors, counselors, and teachers with refined distinctions about the inner life of students, the whole person we are working with, helping us read their behaviors, emotions, and reactions.

Advising and counseling methods over the past few years are merging together. Counseling and advising provides support to people to help them deal with problems and make important decisions, and guides them using a psychological framework. In the *iSuccess* model, advisors are counselors and counselors are advisors, both using the *iSelf* model as the psychological framework to empower students.

To be aware of these methods for counseling students increases student success professionals' effectiveness when transforming students in our care.

Developmental and Intrusive Advising

Arkansas Technical University through its intensive academic advising intentionally aims to coach students to know who they are more thoroughly than typical university academic advising processes. According to Dr. Rene Couture, "faculty and staff need to see their work as investments in students' lives. . . . We need to be more intrusive in our work" (Couture, 2016).

Indeed, intrusive advising, sometimes referred to as "whole-person advising," anticipates the needs of the whole person with a focus on the interests, abilities, and goals of the students, (Glennen, 1975). This requires the ability to see inside the minds of students, to know with more certainty who they are and that they might be going through developmental and life changes.

Proactive advising involves

- deliberate intervention to enhance student motivation,
- using strategies to show interest and involvement with students,
- intensive advising designed to increase the probability of student success,
- working to educate students on all options, and
- approaching students before situations develop.

Additionally, and consistent with Dr. Couture's "intrusive" advising, Dr. Grites, a leading voice in the academic advising profession, advocates for professional advisors to utilize a *developmental advising* approach when working closely with students. This approach is highly compatible with our student success model. According to Dr. Grites, "Developmental academic advising is holistic. The approach includes the education and the development of the whole student (educational, career, and personal) and acknowledges that these dimensions cannot be treated independently, as events in one dimension will often affect another dimension or both of them" (Grites, 2013, p. 12). Both intrusive and developmental advising could benefit from a set of whole-person attributions for academic advisors to focus on. The *iSelf* model can help academic advising professionals add value to both the intrusive and developmental approaches.

Academic advising traditionally takes place in "situations in which an institutional representative gives insight or direction to a college student about an academic, social, or personal matter. The nature of this direction might be to inform, suggest, counsel, discipline, coach, mentor, or even teach" (Grites, 2013, p. 3). Students' needs and their definition of success are at the center of the advising process, rather than the institution's requirements.

Finally, advisors and counselors using developmental and intrusive methods can deepen their transformative impact by focusing on the well-being of students and their quality-of-life visions: "Developmental academic advising is a systematic process based on a close student-advisor relationship intended to aid students in achieving educational, career, and personal goals through the utilization of the full range of institutional and community resources. It both stimulates and supports students in their quest for an enriched quality of life" (Winston et al., 1984, p. 538).

There are two additional methods to use to impart holistic student attributions: coaching and strength-based counseling methods.

Coaching

The coaching method is intended to empower the future personal and professional potentials of students. It is becoming the most effective method for shifting responsibility for a positive life direction because the career, CAPS professional, or academic advisor works closely with the student to define problems and creative solutions. The analogy often used is one from the sport of football, where the quarterback is on the field taking positive actions to win, while the coach is on the sidelines observing and advising. Coaching works because it assumes that people are good and want to manifest their full and unique potentials in life. Additionally, it works because the coach trusts the student's spirit, talents, and motivations to create positive changes toward a future of her choosing. The coaching process places the student and her whole-person needs at the center of counseling and advising sessions and uses personalized and person-centered methods.

Strengths-Based Counseling and Appreciative Inquiry

Strengths-based counseling represents a paradigm shift in counseling and advising methods associated with the similar shift that positive psychology represents. It focuses on what is working in life, in various domains, and how to leverage those positive attributes. For example, a student may have a strong sense of life purpose, a strength, but not be aware of his emotions and how these emotions play out in his relationships.

New academic advising and career counseling models that are strengths based teach students to transform their understanding of who they are in academic and career situations from deficits to strengths. The immediate impact is a new perspective of self. Increased self-esteem occurs almost simultaneously, as does valuing oneself for identified strengths. We are advocating a strengths-based approach to advising: "While compatible with the developmental paradigm, through which advisors concentrate on student growth, the strengths-based approach provides a new lens through which to view students, the academic advising relationship, and the broader college experience. This lens shifts the focus of the advising sessions from areas of need to areas of talent and engagement, and dreams and passions" (Schreiner and Anderson, 2005).

A counselor will focus on this student's life purpose and facilitate a discussion using the *appreciative inquiry* (AI) technique about additional self-attributes or levels of conscious awareness to propel desired life directions. The base assumption is that all healthy, functioning individuals do indeed have positive attributions of which they may not be aware, where having this awareness would empower motivation and energy toward the fulfillment of desired goals and dreams. Strengths-based counseling, life coaching, and advising are focused on future states of mind, reality, and success, versus processing past experiences in order to heal these. As we learned from positive psychology; a common reference is that clients start their therapy from "0" on a scale of "–5 to 0 to +5" in terms of their well-being, with the goal being to achieve in the positive range.

AI is grounded in the premise that identifying and appreciating the strengths already present in an individual or organization can cause them to amplify. An advisor might use AI when working with a student who is having problems with deciding on an academic major. The advisor could discuss student academic weaknesses as potential obstacles to successful degree completion, or (and preferably) inquire about why the student might want a particular degree as a higher purpose to contribute to an issue or problem. This acknowledges the student's innate sense that they are called to do good in the world, a strength to be recognized.

While studying the association and correlation between mental health and disorders and student success in school and life, we have analyzed which of the mental health diagnoses described in the American Psychiatric Association's Diagnostic and Statistics Manual, 4th edition (DSM-IV), could be preventatively addressed through the implementation of the *iSelf* model in either an educative classroom setting or a counseling therapeutic setting.

In one of coauthor Henry's cases handled through his clinical counseling practice, "Mary" had been diagnosed with borderline personality disorder (BPD), which is defined and described by the National Institute of Mental Health (NIMH) as follows: "Borderline personality disorder (BPD) is characterized by pervasive instability in moods, interpersonal relationships, self-image, and behavior. While a person with depression or bipolar disorder typically endures the same mood for weeks, a person with BPD may experience intense bouts of anger, depression, and anxiety that may last for only a few hours to a day" (NIMH, 2011). Certainly these symptoms are common among numerous if not most college-aged students (maybe most often observed just prior to finals).

Through an eight-session learning and treatment plan using AI and the *iSelf* model, and positive psychology attributes in particular, we focused on Mary's self-image, self-esteem, self-schema, self-understanding, emotional understanding of her family dynamics, and purpose and dreams for her life. Mary made a dramatic transformation in her life. She went from being withdrawn and angry with her family to participating in family outings and preparing meals. Additionally, she went on a college visitation tour with her mother, toward whom she had previously shown considerable anxiety and anger. Mary went on to major in philosophy and psychology so as to be able to help children navigate childhood and adolescence successfully—her realized purpose in life.

Mary's BPD symptoms were minimized and addressed at the ontological (being) level, and she has not had repeating symptoms in ten years since the intervention.

There are many more people of all ages, adolescents, young adults, and adults, who are walking around with undiagnosed, untreated borderline personalities. They suffer in silence because BPD is difficult to diagnose and then address with the appropriate intervention or well-being prevention workshop. Every day that goes by is another day adolescents and young adults in our care have not been helped, have not been provided a model of understanding themselves so that they can put into context the complexities of modern life and heal themselves.

Approximately 9.1 percent of the adult US population has been diagnosed with personality disorders. Personality disorders represent "an enduring pattern of inner experience and behavior that deviates markedly from the expectations of the culture of the individual who exhibits it," according to the DSM-IV. These patterns tend to be consistent across varied situations and are typically perceived to be appropriate by the individual, even though they may markedly affect their day-to-day life in negative ways.

What makes these personality disorders so difficult to diagnose, provided with this description, is that all teenagers, when very honest, will indicate that they have either the "inner experience" or "behavior" that "deviates markedly" from their families or "culture," if not for the external behavioral controls established by family, schools, or culture. So, at the inner self, ontological level, to address those inner experiences of difference helps young people feel better about who they are, which leads to improved self-esteem. These disorders encompass antisocial personality disorder, avoidant personality disorder, borderline personality disorder, and emotionally unstable disorder, and are characterized by the lack of one's identity. Erikson (1968; 1980) and Marcia (1966; 1991) would say that this is a normal process—seeking one's identity—at the adolescent stage of development. We would draw your attention to the use of the phrase "inner experience that deviates markedly from the expectations of the culture" as a very gray area in which to clearly diagnose and prescribe a course of action.

Therefore, AI in combination with the *iSelf* attributes is an effective tool to empower new perspectives for success, with clarity based on future dreams and sense of purpose in life, providing preventative counseling to preempt pathologizing a particular symptom whenever possible.

The *iSelf* model attributions serve as an effective framework to assess well-being, guide discussions, and measure results or effectiveness of the intervention, and when appropriate, indicate the need for referrals.

The *iSelf* model attributions form the student success model assessment rubric, which accomplishes two goals: (1) place students at the center of their learning careers and college learning experiences, and, (2) expand our definition of student success from narrow measures of graduation rates to a broader more holistic view. Both add value to the student's experience to prepare the student for a positive life course trajectory filled with flourishing, well-being, and success.

Self Across the Curriculum (*SAC*)

The *Self Across the Curriculum* (*SAC*) is a pedagogy that has been used in college undergraduate and graduate courses to improve student learning outcomes. University faculty have used *SAC* when teaching educational psychology, human development, curriculum and instruction, psychology, motivation, student affairs, and academic advising, among numerous additional courses.

SAC was developed to impart *iSelf* model attributions when we discovered that students were more engaged in learning when it is self-referential, where the self of the student is used as a prism or the lens through which to view all subject content; thus the information learned relates more directly to other situations and employs higher cognitive and metacognitive functions.

The *SAC* teaches students how to first understand themselves, and then how to process and understand the content information that is taught through traditional college courses (e.g., psychology, math, and writing). What results is deeper learning and understanding of both the self and the subject content.

The *SAC* helps faculty

- Increase students' abilities to be more engaged in their learning by applying knowledge.
- Connect students with the content for increased learning outcomes and professional competencies.
- Demonstrate how to develop rigorous academic mind-sets among students.
- Increase connections between students and teachers.
- Help universities score higher on key faculty assessments, such as the National Survey of Student Engagement (NSSE) and Faculty Survey of Student Engagement (FSSE).
- Contribute to the universities' mission to promote student success and well-being through teaching self-knowledge.
- Contribute to a paradigmatic shift in societal values and the greater good.

Just as the popular college Writing across the Curriculum (WAC) has two simultaneous goals, to teach writing skills through content and to use writing to teach subject content, the *SAC* also has two goals: to teach self-knowledge through content and to use self-knowledge to help students connect with the content more thoroughly and deeply. This type of teaching and learning requires a different focus, an internal focus versus an external one; it drives the learner to look inward first, to know one's self and attain a sense of purpose, dreams, moral center, and personal strengths, so as to literally create or construct one's self using the *iSelf* model as a framework. The advantage of learning about the self is that when it is time to develop a strategy to learn about and apply course content, students demonstrate dramatically increased efficacy and creativity when problem solving.

The *SAC* utilizes a contextual teaching and learning method, which connects the content that students are learning (e.g., environmental science) with the context in which that content can be used (e.g., designing a city park and planting trees) and also with attributions of the self in real-world situations—attributions of the self such as self-efficacy, which can be learned through a project-based learning activity. A student can learn that she has a belief that she can accomplish this project as a member of a student group, and that she has a new set of personal beliefs that the environment is important to her. Finally, she discovers that creating new sustainable methods is her true calling professionally, so as to save the planet from global warming.

SAC is a flexible pedagogy that requires faculty to creatively identify and incorporate as many of the *iSelf* self-system and positive psychology attributes as possible to provide personalized learning opportunities.

Connecting Academic Content to the Self

Connecting content with context is an important component part of bringing meaning to the learning process and making learning more personalized. Further, *SAC*'s intent is to access the natural learning system that all students possess—learning about one's self—as this is one's first interest.

The self-schema component of the *iSelf* model is critical to learning and growing and developing as a person through academic courses and all learning environments, and it is important for educators and mental and physical health service providers, and all those committed to student success, to use it in their work. Leading self-referential scholars underscore this view: "In order for self-reference to be such a useful encoding process, the self must be a uniform, well-structured concept. During the recall phase of the study, subjects probably use the self as a retrieval cue" (Moscovitch and Craik, 1976).

"In order for [self-reference] to be functional, the self must be a consistent and uniform schema" (Rogers, Kuiper, and Kirker, 1977, p. 686).

In two experiments, incidental recall of rated words indicated that adjectives rated under the self-reference task were recalled the best. These results indicate that self-reference is a rich and powerful encoding process. As an aspect of the human information-processing system, the self appears to function as a superordinate schema that is deeply involved in the processing, interpretation, and memory of personal information (Rogers, Kuiper, and Kirker, 1977, p. 677).

University professors pride themselves on producing the next great mind in a particular field, someone who can create new ideas and approaches in professional pursuit. All academic disciplines are required to make certain that what they teach is aligned with a set of professional standards, and that students are measured on these as learning outcomes. We argue that if deeper learning is one of the results of good teaching, and that students also learn new visions for professional success through course assignments, what faculty member wouldn't utilize *SAC*?

Faculty can also help provide deeper learning opportunities that integrate doing and reflection and are tied to academic objectives. Personal and professional competencies are gained through real-world learning experiences and engaged scholarship. Their focus is on developing an important student success competency, that of an *academic mind-set*. This is of particular importance to faculty members:

> In addition to motivating a student's engagement in deeper learning instructional practices, positive academic mind-sets can also be seen as important deeper learning outcomes. The outcomes of academic programs are not only content knowledge and academic competencies, but also the people that students become from having participated in their educational experiences. To develop young adults with a positive and efficacious sense of self and confidence in their abilities to engage with and contribute to the world, universities need to provide deeper learning opportunities in which students can follow their interests, strengthen bonds with peers, collaborate with a diverse range of people, build their competence over time, and come to see that accomplishment is built upon sustained hard work (Farrington, 2013).

SAC Helps Achieve NSSE and FSSE Results

Universities are measured using the National Survey of Student Engagement (NSSE) survey of student satisfaction, and faculty are evaluated in part using the Faculty Survey of Student Engagement (FSSE); however, all frontline educators and advisors can also greatly influence these outcomes. They are measured on the quality of the classroom teaching and the quality of the relationship with students, either as a mentor or advisor.

More and more students' voices are emerging as driving forces for positive changes.

Interactions with faculty can positively influence the cognitive growth, development, and persistence of college students. Through their formal and informal roles as teachers, advisors, and mentors, faculty members' model intellectual works to promote mastery of knowledge and skills, and help students make connections between their studies and their future plans. The FSSE asks students to evaluate interactions with faculty and respond to this series of questions:

During the current school year, how often have you
- Talked about career plans with a faculty member?
- Worked with a faculty member on activities other than course work (committees, student groups, etc.)?
- Discussed course topics, ideas, or concepts with a faculty member outside of class?
- Discussed your academic performance with a faculty member?

Student views are also being valued as they relate to *Reflective and Integrative Learning* measures. Personally connecting with course material requires students to relate their understandings and experiences to the content at hand. Instructors emphasizing reflective and integrative learning motivate students to make connections between their learning and the world around them, reexamining their own beliefs and considering issues and ideas from others' perspectives. Items include the following:

During the current school year, how often have you
- Combined ideas from different courses when completing assignments?
- Connected your learning to societal problems or issues?
- Included diverse perspectives (political, religious, racial/ethnic, gender, etc.) in course discussions or assignments?

- Examined the strengths and weaknesses of your own views on a topic or issue?
- Tried to better understand someone else's views by imagining how an issue looks from his or her perspective?
- Learned something that changed the way you understand an issue or concept?
- Connected ideas from your courses to your prior experiences and knowledge?

Questions are from the copyrighted NSSE and FSSE surveys and reproduced with permission.

The nature of these questions requires that students understand the integration of academic content with career direction, in one example, or changing personal beliefs and increasing self-understanding in another. Therefore, faculty and frontline educators need to build into their courses opportunities to reference student learning, raise the conscious awareness of students, and tie growth and development back to these measures to inform their own effectiveness in course design.

Margaret W. Cohen, Associate Provost for Professional Development and Director of the Center for Teaching and Learning, University of Missouri–St. Louis states the importance of the FSSE: "We rely upon NSSE and FSSE data to encourage the campus community to take responsibility for student learning and engagement."

As an example of the growing interest in student success promising practices to improve NSSE and Community College Survey of Student Engagement (CCSSE) measures, the Minnesota State colleges and universities system convened member campuses for a two-day working conference to build upon efforts to promote promising practices for student success—practices aligned with the chancellor's priorities to dramatically increase student retention, successful transfer, and completion of degrees. Sessions addressed practices (learning communities, service learning, first-year seminars, and undergraduate research) for both state university and two-year college student success (CCSSE, 2014).

The goal of the conference was to use data, including results from NSSE and CCSSE, "to inform the design of such practices, with particular emphasis on first-year experience courses, supplemental instruction, and accelerated developmental education" (NSSE, 2013, p. 28).

We hope to inform educators and the NSSE and CCSSE to enhance their surveys with an integrated view and to develop questions that address well-being and holistic student needs. The value the *iSelf* model and *SAC* offer faculty members is that they have a way to appreciate the mind-sets of their students, a framework to better understand what is going on with their students, internally. Much like what the Theory of Multiple Intelligences (MI) did for helping teachers understand additional ways to reach students based upon learning styles or strengths, so too the *iSelf* model expands these abilities even further.

We would highlight that it is important to include the *iSelf* model, *SAC*, and *Success Predictor* as additional high-impact practices that address *student* perspectives of success, and ways to teach these to further improve survey results.

Far more easily than they realize, faculty can readily integrate the self of their students in teaching and learning through numerous course lessons.

Faculty Learning about Mental Health and Well-Being

A preventative education program at the University of Pennsylvania's counseling and psychological services department, the I CARE program, offers an intensive and interactive seven-hour training to learn the signs of distress and mental health crises that can affect students.

Since March 2014, the I CARE programs have trained 410 faculty and staff members at 13 events. Four hundred students have been trained at seven events. What is important for us to consider for our student success model is that faculty and staff are more involved, committed to and integrated into the life and success of each student. What is needed in this program as with others that attempt to prevent incidences is a comprehensive model that can be used immediately by students to resolve their stressors in life and begin the healing process. This type of program that intervenes into a student's mind-set and associated dynamics is known as a psycho-education program.

Higher education CAPS departments are attempting to train more faculty members, where 64 percent increased the amount of time in training faculty and others to respond helpfully to students in difficulty and to make appropriate referrals (73 percent at large schools; NSCC, 2014, p. 6).

The *iSelf* model, as taught through the *SAC*, helps us to first process the abundant information required to live in modern society and then transform ourselves to achieve higher levels of consciousness. Through this heightened consciousness, we can move toward the person we want to become and, more directly, are meant to be.

Student-Centered Personalized Learning

Once faculty and other professionals understand the ideas behind this approach, they can use the strategy in the classroom, aligning students' academic learning with what they are learning in co-curricular activities, and through career and personal counseling. The ideas can be incorporated into the development and delivery of personalized learning plans across all academic subjects, helping students become more engaged learners.

Personalized learning holds the promise to focus on the whole person—those psychological and physical well-being needs of each young adult—with the aim of full and unique potential for a high-quality life. Because these goals are not mutually exclusive, it could also satisfy the educational aims of our society to see people graduate from college, get a job, and participate in our democracy—all while addressing critical well-being needs.

If our educational aims explicitly reflect our well-being, societal needs, and such 21st-century needs as interpersonal and intrapersonal skills, communication skills, leadership skills, and higher-order cognitive skills (e.g., problem solving and creativity), then we should define the most effective framework and model to get there.

An ideal personalized learning plan (PLP) is developed using the *iSelf* model through *SAC*, in which student self-knowledge is elevated to a higher role and framework to formulate educational experiences that are aligned with student purpose and dreams.

What is often missing in personalized learning is the ability to take a deeper look at the inner self of the learner, to know who they are and want to become. Therefore, the focus of personalized learning should be on each student's needs across all domains: social, emotional, physical, and academic. A personalized learning program should enable students to do the following:

- Maintain high standards of mental and physical health and well-being, learning lifelong methods to further develop this well-being
- Become ready for college, career, and life, demonstrating numerous competencies in each domain
- Become self-confident members of their community, contributing to the greater societal good
- Know themselves and their strengths, weaknesses, and future hopes and dreams
- Have the flexibility to learn in both traditional and nontraditional ways, in and outside of the classroom, to support their unique strengths and needs

A true student-centered focus requires that we tailor lessons not only to a student's abilities, interests, and preferences but also to the self-components and attributes of the *iSelf* model—future life dreams, self-esteem, emotional intelligence, and the others we discussed earlier in the chapter.

By using this approach to focus on the balance of psychological and physical well-being, students' academic achievement and overall quality of life are destined to improve.

Further, personalized learning will allow our higher education institutions to accommodate the goal of learning in and out of the classroom through co-curricular opportunities such as independent study, internships, private instruction, performing groups, community service (service-learning), and online instruction. If we are able to truly personalize learning in these ways, students will take control of their own learning and responsibility for their life-course trajectories—their own success.

The *Success Predictor* (*SP*): For Academic, Career, and Life Direction

The *Success Predictor* is a diagnostic and assessment instrument and intervention tool that raises the conscious awareness of college students as to their responsibilities to create their own definition of student success, and the pathways to achieve it.

The *Success Predictor* is a highly effective tool used by student success professionals to help guide people of all ages, developmental stages, and walks of life toward their highest expressions of what is possible for them. It can be used simply to help students establish goals and identify with passions. But it is more deeply effective when used to assess, diagnose, and intervene into the mind-set of people who want to see and achieve their full and unique potentials life—empowering them to succeed and manifest their full and unique potentials.

The *Success Predictor* is typically used to

- determine internal motivations to succeed,
- understand reference points of capabilities,
- diagnose internal states of well-being,
- formulate career aspirations,
- determine professional acumen,
- understand academic program interests,
- guide college selection and fit,

- guide life and career directions,
- understand personal paradigms of reality,
- guide interventions,
- and more.

The *Success Predictor* is used to help guide students when making a transformation from the person they think they are *supposed* to be to the person they know they are *meant* to be. From a student's perspective, a college learning career with numerous experiences offers a special opportunity, most likely for the first time in their lives, to reflect upon "Who am I now?" and "How have my life circumstances shaped me to be the person I am *supposed* to be?" These circumstances may be: family values, childhood trauma(s), traditions, behaviors, and dominant cultural forces (such as the Great Recession, "9/11," social media, prevalence of prescription drugs, mass school shootings, and global warming, among others). Students can reflect on "Who am I *meant* to be, now that I am on my own?" Special and unique is the opportunity to consider life purpose. "Do I have a calling in life, repressed dreams for my life?" and "What is meaningful to me?" are among the important questions to ask at this developmental stage.

If a student reveals personal challenges and emotional issues beyond the scope of the advisor's role or expertise, advisors and counselors should be prepared to refer them to the appropriate licensed professional for additional counseling or guidance. However, most students find the *Success Predictor* empowering and uplifting on their pathway to success.

New student orientation workshops, first-year transition programs, CAPS promoting well-being workshops, career services workshops, academic advising for undeclared students, among numerous other applications of the *Success Predictor* can help empower student success.

Handbook for Administering the *Success Predictor*

Student success professionals can administer the *SP* in a variety of settings, such as new student orientation workshops, first-year transition programs, counseling and psychological services well-being prevention workshops, career services workshops, academic advising for undeclared students assessing program fit, and faculty advising sessions, among others.

Instructions for Advisors, Counselors, and Faculty

In preparation for administering the *SP*, please familiarize yourself with the following questions and quotations, and how you might use them to interact with your students in order to establish the appropriate reflective context. (Please feel free to use your own that have inspired you personally and/or professionally.)

Questions to Support Your Inquiry

1. Why is constructivism and positive psychology important for people to study and apply?
2. How does a student/client/person actually "construct" a self? How does this self-construct serve as a valuable framework to design pathways to success during the college learning career and beyond in life?
3. In which ways does a person's level of consciousness impact the ability to construct knowledge about one's self?
4. How do we convey that education is a journey about how to achieve the good life, with mental and physical well-being, flourishing, and success?
5. Is the degree to which a student/person can construct a self-concept and a self-system important to academic learning excellence, life satisfaction, and well-being?

Quotes to Support Your Inquiry

"Dream up a good life!"

Jim Carrey

"Some men see things as they are and say why. I dream things that never were and say, why not?"

Robert F. Kennedy

"To both Piaget and Erikson, the person does not become a true individual or personality until he has integrated his thoughts and feelings about himself into a total life perspective which expands beyond personal interest to the whole of mankind."

David Elkind, in *Six Psychological Studies* by Jean Piaget

"Subject-object theory brings together two powerful lines of intellectual discourse that have influenced not only the field of psychology but nearly every corner of intellectual life in the West in this century. These two lines of thought are constructivism, the idea that people or systems constitute or construct reality; and developmentalism, the idea that people or organic systems evolve through qualitatively different eras of increasing complexity according to regular principles of stability and change."

Robert Kegan, In Over Our Heads

"Our minds, in reflecting on what we see, endow these images with separate identities, identities they have only in our imagination. This is the process of reification, by which we attribute reality to mental constructions. The self is such a reification, and certainly one of the most significant ones. We usually think of it as a force, a spark, an inner flame with an indivisible integrity. Yet, from what we know now, the self is more in the nature of a figment of the imagination, something we create to account for the multiplicity of impressions, emotions, thoughts, and feelings that the brain records in consciousness."

Mihaly Csikszentmihalyi, The Evolving Self

The *Success Predictor* is a questionnaire to be completed by a person searching for what is next—in life transitions, academic interests, and career transitions, for improved quality of life. The questionnaire helps both the student and the professional understand the important connections among personal life purpose and dreams, professional and career aspirations, academic interests and academic program selection, education or professional credentials strategy formulation, and internships and service learning strategies.

The following step-by-step instructions are written from the student's point of view; therefore, references to "your" or "your personal situation" are intended for students.

Instructions for Students

Please review and become familiar with the categories and the definitions used in the *Success Predictor*. You and your advisor/counselor/life coach/student success coach will inquire into a new possibility and what is possible for you in your life.

Review the following pages and become familiar with the word definitions or categories used in the *Success Predictor*. Also, become familiar with the questions posed within each word category. Word definitions are provided as well as questions that assist you in formulating a personal connection to the word category. For purposes of completing the *Success Predictor* questionnaire, each word category is a level of your consciousness, your own knowing about you and the way you frame your reality. Therefore, it is important that you take each word category and develop a personal experience of it, or derive personal meaning.

Please take the ten word distinctions or categories and view them as a hierarchy or levels of understanding. The ten word distinctions below are not ordered by level; therefore, please organize them by level, much like solving a puzzle, which assists in the transformation of how you organize your own view of reality and self. You may need to make a number of attempts to organize the distinctions to solve the puzzle. There is no absolute correct puzzle solution, but there is a *best* solution for you that most accurately represents your hierarchy of consciousness.

Levels of understanding means that one category requires a higher level of understanding or broader view than another does. Therefore, when formulating your response to the category such as "purpose," please consider where that category ranks in your level of understanding.

Remember, when you have completed the questionnaire, this is a snapshot or present picture of who you are and your view of your reality, self, and future success, so please consider your responses carefully and consciously.

Often, participants using the *Success Predictor* take pictures cut out of magazines or photographs of their life and paste them into a workbook. These pictures assist in clarifying what each level of understanding looks and feels like. Please do not use your public social media spaces to post your workbook pictures; keep these private during your participation. You may upon completion of your participation post all of the pictures as well as your results.

Your responses in each category may be in written and/or picture form.

As previously mentioned, the *Success Predictor* has ten categories. These are currently in no particular order:

Categories

Results. Evidence that you are on the right track toward manifesting your purpose, vision, goals, and plans; a compass; what occurs after you take action.

Mission. An inner calling to pursue an activity or perform a service; a vocation; the area of life where you will manifest your life's purpose.

Commitments. What you are determined to do; a pledge to do something; a state of being bound emotionally or intellectually to someone or something, like a strong belief.

Being. The essence of a human being; the totality of all things that exist; the qualities that constitute existence or essence; one's basic nature.

Tactics. Step-by-step actions to take to implement your plans; a series of steps toward achieving a goal or implementing a plan.

Goals. To accomplish something by a certain time; "what by when."

Vision. What you can see in the future; a dream of what is possible; a mental image produced by the imagination, to see in your mind's eye; unusual competence or perception; intelligent foresight.

Strategies. An approach to take, or method to use to accomplish a specific goal; how you will manifest your goals; approaches or alternatives.

Plans. To form a scheme or program for the accomplishment of a goal; to make a graphic representation, like a blueprint; how you will execute the strategies formulated.

Purpose. The reason why you are here, for your existence; raison d'être; describes or includes your basic nature or being.

Notes: (1) When completing your responses to these categories, please use as much space as required, or as many pages as you want; (2) Brief definitions and examples are provided in each category to assist you in formulating your own understandings; (3) Source of definitions: *The American Heritage College Dictionary*.

Review and Analysis

Once you have completed the *Success Predictor* hierarchy to your satisfaction, review it with your advisor, counselor, and/or teachers. Discuss your view and justify why you placed a word at a particular level. Your advisor, counselor, or teacher will reveal the typical placement of word distinctions and the complete hierarchy, and then compare and contrast differences or similarities with your interpretation, not to change yours, but to highlight categories of importance to you.

You may decide to bring to your sessions the workbook of pictures you collected that visually represent your views. This often allows for an engaging and very personal conversation. Therefore, if you do not feel comfortable engaging in this type of discussion, then you can opt out of this discussion.

Suggestions for Advisors, Counselors, and Faculty

Advisors, counselors, and faculty should note and assess students' responses for each level in their hierarchy, and consider whether or not they have thoroughly responded and understood each level, and where they could use additional coaching support. Advisors and counselors should always place the responsibility for understanding and expanding their responses on the students, as they are the ones creating a self and their pathway to the success they envision.

The initial introduction or final review of the *Success Predictor* results can take place in either a one-on-one format or group process. This introduction and final review works very well in class group discussions, or in small discussion groups/pods in, for example, new student orientation sessions. The final review and completion of the *Success Predictor* is best done on a private, individual basis, as it is a very introspective and personal process.

How the *Success Predictor* Works

Emotions are important because they motivate us to grow and develop and make a difference in the world—the real world. Without emotions and motivated reasoning, change is not possible. When a client or student knows what she wants, and she is passionate about it for whatever reason, structural tension is created. *Structural tension* is a clinical term to describe the energy created when an individual concurrently envisions a desired future state, while being completely aware of the limitations of present or current reality. The difference between the desired future state and current reality creates a tension that seeks resolution toward one or the other. The idea of structural tension applies the first axiom of structural dynamics (Odum, 1988) to individual change. In any counseling or teaching relationship, it is critical to establish this structural tension in order to empower positive change. When this tension is created, emotional thought drives the change process. As educators and counselors, it is our responsibility to guide positive changes and provide tools or methods so that students can learn how to do this for themselves.

The *Success Predictor* uses the first axiom of structural dynamics (Odum, 1988) that tension seeks resolution (Figure 5). This initiates the change process—the emotional desire to attain a future state, a goal, a dream. This axiom is essential for all student success professionals to understand and apply to university-based curricula, counseling programs, and mental and physical health programs.

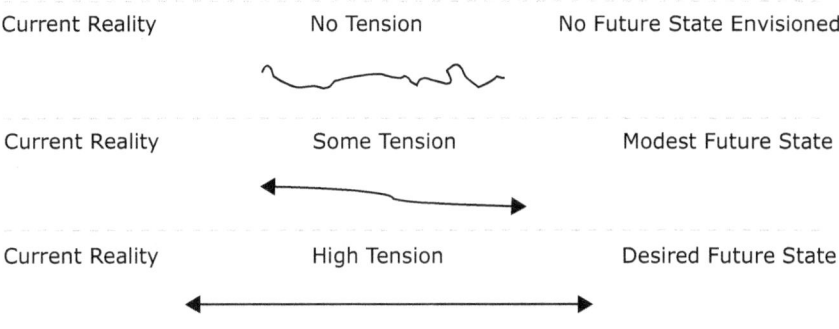

Figure 5. Structural Tension in High-Impact Student Success Practices

Figure 5 presents three levels of tension between the left side, current reality, and the right side, the degree to which a future state is desired. The first level is "No Tension," which indicates that a person is just going through the motions, floating through life, allowing circumstances to dictate direction and feelings, and sense of self, with very little commitment toward anyone or anything, including self and personal growth and development. Additionally, the person does not have a clear picture of present reality, either emotional states or physical situation. The second level, "Moderate Tension," indicates a modest commitment to a desired future state, most often with the ability to envision general circumstances such as more money, new car, or better relationships. Most likely this person is not able to envision a future state that includes emotions or to feel as an important part of the quality of life. This person is also not very clear about his or her present emotional state.

The third level, "High Tension," indicates the ability to dream about a complete and whole picture that includes emotional states of being, who one wants to become (e.g., a good person who makes a difference), and numerous and clear distinctions about both emotional and circumstantial future realities. This person also clearly identifies current emotional states, even if they include sadness or frustration that the future state is yet to be realized. This person also is clearer about unique potential in life—something special that he or she has to give or contribute to others.

Helping students understand who they are and their own pathways to success in college and later in life happens through effective counseling and teaching that changes minds and brains in the same way and through the same pathway—the integrated self of the person in our care. In both settings, we are changing behaviors through changing thoughts and feelings that impact the neural networks in our brains. When a student or patient is learning, all these are at work; all are changing simultaneously. As such, as counselors and teachers, we need to be aware of and responsible for our interventions, as they are impacting the self of the students at deep, fundamental levels.

Students already know that they want something, to be a better person, to be successful, to change the world in their unique manner. They have self-interest in attending college. As frontline educators, faculty, academic advisors, and personal and career counselors, we need to be aware that students have an internal drive, or intrinsic motivations fueled by emotions.

We draw upon the breakthrough work in mind, brain, and education (MBE) for a deeper look into students' inner dynamics: "The processes of recognizing and responding to complex situations, which we suggest hold the origins of creativity, are fundamentally emotional and social. As such, they are shaped by and evaluated within a cultural context and are based upon emotional processing. No matter how complex and esoteric they become, our repertoire of behavioral and cognitive options continues to exist in the service of emotional goals" (Immordino-Yang and Damasio, 2007, p. 7). In sum, everything we do for ourselves or for others serves the self at some or many levels.

It is the self of the individual that engages in learning experiences that marry emotions with thinking to arrive at an outcome, a result from the learning experience. All learning is dedicated toward achieving goals that emphasize the personal and social domains. The self mediates between the social and the personal, and the external with the internal. We make conscious decisions to place ourselves in particular situations where we are called upon to learn, to express, and to add to the interactive dynamics of the interpsychological and intrapsychological processes required to succeed or manifest our goal. Damasio's "collection of systems dedicated to goal-oriented thinking" reinforces the view that reasoning toward the manifestation of a dream considers both personal and social interests, not an either/or perspective. Said another way, inherently, at the "being" level as human beings, we strive to produce positive outcomes for both ourselves and others.

Final Thoughts

The three high-impact student success practices discussed in this chapter represent the most complete approaches to placing students at the center of creating selves, with pathways to their own definitions of success. These definitions and pathways to success on their terms offer students the opportunity to create possible selves that manifest their highest hopes and dreams for great lives filled with accomplishment, deep personal and professional satisfaction, and emotional and psychological well-being.

In the next chapter, we discuss examples of how these high-impact practices can be infused across all five functions in the *iSuccess* model, along with promising practices from numerous colleges and universities from across America.

CHAPTER 6

STUDENT SUCCESS IN PRACTICE

The *iSuccess* model requires integration of the higher education student success functions—academic advising, career services, counseling and psychological services (CAPS), faculty teaching, and student engagement.

In this chapter, we have included numerous submissions of promising practices from some of the most innovative professionals in their respective fields, representing many types of higher education institutions. (Recall as well that some additional promising practices were included in Chapter 3 to enhance the discussion on higher education's changing mission.) The reader will see that these promising practices begin to represent aspects of the *iSuccess* model. We map these promising practices to the *iSuccess* model and the three student success high-impact practices, as well as discuss the ways the functional areas can work together. Finally, we have included some of our own examples, which we call *high-impact practices* in that they directly use the principles and practices of the *iSuccess* model.

Our intention is that the reader will find these examples of both promising and high-impact practices useful as a handbook of how to implement and raise awareness of the *iSuccess* model.

The *iSuccess* model can be used by a wide array of Carnegie classified (2015) institutions of higher education, such as:

- Doctoral universities—Highest, higher, modest research activity (R1), (R2), (R3)
- Master's colleges and universities—Larger, medium, smaller programs (M1), (M2), (M3)
- Baccalaureate colleges—Arts and sciences, diverse fields, associates dominant, mixed

- Associates colleges—High transfer traditional, high transfer mixed traditional/nontraditional, high transfer nontraditional, mixed transfer/career, among others
- Special focus two- and four-year schools

The three high-impact practices, the *Integrated Self* model (*iSelf*), *Self Across the Curriculum* (*SAC*), and *Success Predictor* (*SP*), are equally effective in all of the various types of schools because they focus on the student as a whole person.

As higher education institutions are realizing the importance of restructuring around the student and student success functions, student success is fast becoming a distinct body of work, with separate professional and student practices. We hope that the examples presented serve both students and professionals more thoroughly. We want you to be successful to the level of your own hopes and dreams.

Teaching

Faculty have numerous opportunities to impart self-knowledge and empower students to develop their own definitions of success as a part of teaching and learning or through one-on-one advising sessions. Faculty have long searched for ways to help empower students to be more self-directed, and to take initiatives and intellectual risks when thinking about important issues and concerns. To shift responsibility for learning of any kind, personal or intellectual, from teacher to student is a common goal. The shift in teaching and learning methods is commonly known as going from "sage on the stage" to "coach on the side" and helps students take more responsibility in their classroom and throughout their college learning careers.

We have shown how the *Self Across the Curriculum* (*SAC*) is the breakthrough needed to produce young people who are academically, cognitively, and emotionally prepared to meet 21st-century demands.

Promising Practice:
Fostering Self-Direction through First-Year Seminars

Many schools now build into the curriculum first-year seminars or other programs that bring small groups of students together with faculty or staff on a regular basis. The highest-quality first-year experiences place a strong emphasis on critical inquiry, frequent writing, information literacy, collaborative learning, and other skills that develop students' intellectual and practical competencies. First-year seminars can also involve students with cutting-edge questions in scholarship and with faculty members' own research.

A promising practice at Butler County Community College involves integrating student affairs with academic divisions to help students understand that they are required to be self-directed in every aspect of their college experience.

At Butler County Community College, leaders realized the importance of an integrated model of student success. When developing their student success approach, they began with "student needs," then looked at what internal professional resources would be required to support them. The college then designed new delivery systems and supports to assist students and key functional personnel. More than twenty faculty are involved with Welcome Days and throughout the first full year of a student's transition. Stress and time management workshops are offered as well as opportunities to explore career options and engagement activities. Used with permission from Dr. Case Willoughby and Butler County Community College.

> The orientation process at BC3 was changed dramatically for the 2013–2014 year by a Student Services working group, incorporating feedback from academic divisions and others. Rather than attempting to orient students in a single event just before the start of classes, the committee began to think of orientation as a process that begins at admission and ends in the first semester.
>
> The process was branded "Orientation@BC3: Steps to Success." These "steps" would include a blog (www.bc3stepstosuccess.com), advising and registration (ACE), and Welcome Day—the event just prior to classes.
>
> Using feedback from multiple campus stakeholders, their own experience, and student success research, the committee created learning outcomes for orientation. They include:
> - Students will value their own role in their success (personal responsibility).
> - Students will know the time expectations of college level study (time management).
> - Students will check e-mail frequently.
> - Students will take steps to explore major and career options.
> - Students will know how to navigate the portal.
> - Students will recognize the value of being engaged with the curriculum and co-curriculum (Willoughby, 2015).

The *iSuccess* model aligns with the college's communication with students that they are responsible for creating their own pathway of success that includes academic program selection, career fit, emotional engagement in curricula and co-curricular activities, and personal responsibility to drive their own growth and development.

Students are encouraged to make a promise during their orientation at Butler County Community College: "I will take charge of my education, seek assistance when I need it, and offer to help my fellow students. I will dedicate the time and effort my academics deserves. I will persevere while maintaining the highest ethical standards. I will find ways to get involved in BC3 and contribute to a vibrant community. This is my path to success" (2016b). Under the leadership of Dr. Case Willoughby (2015; 2016a; 2016b), Butler County Community College shifts the responsibility to students to create their own pathways to success, and then measures students' understanding through a survey gauging student reaction to this statement: "As a result of Welcome Day, I know that it's my responsibility to explore major and career goals." This survey resulted in 99.38 percent of students either strongly agreeing or agreeing with this statement and hence learning outcome. This is an example of a community college teaching students to understand that they are responsible for their future success at college that will serve them beyond.

Students reported gains in learning about academic expectations and their own role in their success. Student responses included:

- "As a result of Welcome Day, I know that it's my responsibility to explore major and career goals." (97 percent responded "agree" or "strongly agree.")
- "[Welcome Day] calmed a lot of my fears and helped me feel more confident about starting at BC3" (indicating that students felt a sense of belonging, where hope and new possibilities replaced fear).

During a typical first-year seminar, students are instructed by faculty on how to survive their first year, what to expect in terms of social activities and peer pressure, and how to access tutorial services, financial aid, and student support services such as CAPS.

We suggest that administering the *Success Predictor* to incoming freshmen would empower them to understand that college is a place to create a "new you," to take charge of one's own destiny in life, to build a mental framework necessary to select their academic programs along with internships and co-curricular activities, and to be self-directed when improving their emotional, psychological, and physical well-being.

When faculty engage in inquiry with students, the strategic questions they pose require students to formulate their opinions or points of view. Activities and assignments can help students make connections to other bodies of knowledge or other subjects in their major, such as a foundational course in their discipline in which basic information is used to think critically about ethical implications for society.

When students are asked to think about their own views, they examine their personal paradigms of reality, unconscious beliefs, values, emotional reactions to specific issues, and ethical positions. They may also be inspired and compelled to take action to impact a condition or problem in our society. Here they are connecting to their own hopes and dreams, while developing the self-efficacy necessary to make a difference. Faculty offer opportunities for personal growth through course materials and pedagogical approaches. Students change the way they understand a concept as they change who they are; simultaneously they are changing who they are by understanding a concept newly.

There is a dynamic between academic outcomes and the self-system and positive psychology attributes. If faculty better understand and focus on these attributes as outcomes through curricula, then their students will be more successful in academic schooling outcomes and well-being outcomes. In this process, the teacher is teaching a whole person, not merely the intellect. Therefore, academic outcomes are no more important than well-being outcomes when empowering the full potential of students, and they are not mutually exclusive.

Using this high-impact student success practice results in deeper learning and engagement and new perspectives on definitions of success and pathways to achieve.

Promising Practice: Student Success Course

Title: Emotionally Intelligent Leadership: Concepts and Considerations

Credit: This course was developed by Matthew R. Shupp, EdD, NCC, DCC, Assistant Professor, Coordinator, College Counseling and College Student Personnel Specializations, Department of Counseling and College Student Personnel, College of Education and Human Services, Shippensburg University of Pennsylvania

Student Success Functional Areas: Faculty Teaching / Student Engagement and Learning

History, Rationale, and Significance of Course

Dr. Shupp first developed *Emotionally Intelligent Leadership (EIL): Concepts and Considerations* for the winter term 2014 as an elective within the

Department of Counseling and College Student Personnel, primarily serving students within the College Student Personnel specialization with the goal of meeting the students' required leadership elective. The course aligns with the department's mission of emphasizing personal growth and encouraging "each student to gain competencies, values, and beliefs that will enhance and facilitate the helping process" (para. 1, n.d.). Students develop the knowledge and skills necessary to be purposeful, effective practitioners as they analyze their personal and professional identity. Twelve students enrolled in the course. It was offered once again during the winter term 2015; the course was so popular that it was overenrolled and had a wait-list of students.

Course Description
This course is designed to introduce students to key components integral to successful leadership. Leadership ebbs and flows in time, space, and context. Knowledge of leadership theory and communication styles as well as self-assessment and development is a necessary and continual process for leaders. Students will be asked to examine their own emotionally intelligent leadership, strengths and weaknesses and to begin to make adjustments in their behaviors and attitudes as they experience and examine individuals and organizations that may be, at times, significantly different from their own life experience.

As the course description suggests, Dr. Shupp designed EIL to introduce participants to fundamental emotional intelligence processes with learning outcomes focused on the following:

- Explore the three tenets of emotional intelligence (EI; consciousness of self, consciousness of others, and consciousness of context), as well as the nineteen capacities embedded within self, others, and context.
- Develop a greater awareness of one's EI strengths and areas for growth.
- Appreciate the importance of EI and its impact on teams and the supervisory relationship.

Course Overview
The course was specifically designed and offered during the winter term, with five weekly modules introduced in stepwise progression. Textbook topics were discussed and supported via supplemental articles, lectures, and videos. Weekly discussion boards advanced the conversation from the previous week's learning.

To introduce the course, Dr. Shupp presented an introductory webinar which explained the overall course design and expectations. Likewise, the course was uniquely and purposefully planned with eight hours of face-to-face contact (two days, four hours per day) utilized at the end of the first and fourth weeks of the winter term. Meeting at the conclusion of the first week allowed students to clarify questions as well as the group to coalesce. Coming back together at the end of the fourth week offered students the opportunity to make meaning of the course concepts and synthesize and integrate the online modules into their professional practice.

Comprehensive Nature of the Syllabus
Dr. Shupp utilized a variety of assessments in this course, including face-to-face participation, online discussion boards, a reflection/synthesis theory paper, an emotionally intelligent learning styles inventory, a companion workbook, and a group project.

Students were required to write one leadership paper using emotionally intelligent leadership as their theoretical framework. The paper asked students to identify their strengths as well as areas of growth as identified from their EIL inventory and to address the added benefit of acknowledging emotional intelligence in their professional work.

Collaborative Efforts That Foster Teaching and Learning among Students
Students were assigned to a group where they analyzed a movie through an EIL lens. Creativity abounded as students chose such films as *Toy Story, Brave, Inside Out, Finding Nemo*, and *The Karate Kid*. The students used a wiki package within D2L (the university's learning management system) for seamless online editing of the projects in real time. This collaborative effort on the group project had a secondary benefit, as it allowed group members to assess their own emotional intelligence (from their EIL styles inventory) when working with others.

Student Learning and Feedback
Anonymous feedback was compiled at the completion of the course, and comments from students were generally positive. Students enjoyed the content of the in-person meetings as well as the layout of the online components, the enjoyment in the variety of assessments, the overall pace of the course, as well as the group project. Some of the more compelling comments are below:

> I really enjoyed completing the wiki. This was probably the best group project, as far as satisfaction with working with others, and the ability to be creative and have fun while applying class concepts.

I also enjoyed the in-class sessions with the inventory, as well as the workbook. There was a lot of application to the real world, so it was not as though we were reading theory without immediate or meaningful application.

The course was highly effective due to the amount of application to real-world use (inventory, workbook, wiki, discussion posts—all centered around using the theory). Without the application part of the course, this would not have suited our department as much (anyone can read and synthesize theories). But with the application, I took away the same amount of knowledge, awareness, and skills from this class as others, if not more due to the content.

This course sets an example for integrating the selves of students into academic content. When creating the course and while teaching, Dr. Shupp focuses on self attributes to help students understand the importance and relevancy of these attributes in their future careers and lives. He effectively links self attributes as he discusses academic course content material. This is the Self Across the Curriculum in action. Recall that one of the key processes in the SAC is the self-referential process. This course integrates faculty teaching with student engagement into a seamless experience for each student, imparting personal and professional competencies critical to student success during and after college.

Students take the Emotionally Intelligent Leadership for Students Inventory (Shankman, Allen, and Miguel, 2015), which provides a baseline regarding their level of emotional intelligence, and refer to this assessment tool throughout the duration of the course.

Dr. Shupp teaches the following capacities:

Self—Being aware of yourself in terms of your abilities and emotions
- Emotional self-perception
- Emotional self-control
- Authenticity
- Healthy self-esteem
- Flexibility
- Optimism
- Initiative
- Achievement

Others—Being aware of your relationship with others and the role they play in the leadership equation
- Displaying empathy
- Inspiring others

- Coaching others
- Capitalizing on difference
- Developing relationships
- Building teams
- Demonstrating citizenship
- Managing conflict
- Facilitating change

Context—The environment in which leaders and followers work
- Analyzing the group
- Assessing the environment

Please note the similarity between these capacities and the attributions in our *iSelf* model: self-esteem, emotional intelligence, personal and professional identities, possible selves, hope and dreams, locus of control, and results, among others.

Students are highly engaged in their own learning because they have a personal and professional investment in learning about their own emotions and being more able to lead others in a professional setting with these understandings.

Used with permission from Dr. Matthew Shupp and Shippensburg University of Pennsylvania.

High-Impact Practice: Teaching with *Self Across the Curriculum*

Lesson Activity: "Learning Literacy through the Self: Learning the Self through Literacy"

Coauthor Henry developed this lesson activity for his students at Clarion University, and it was used in Educational Psychology and Human Development and Learning courses.

Lesson Goals

This lesson introduces the central issues in development of the self through literacy—and learning literacy through the self—during the early childhood stages of human development. Students will develop and demonstrate an ability to teach literacy concepts to children and to empower children's self-understanding through a developmentally appropriate lesson activity.

Resources
Students will be asked to draw upon: chapters 9, 10, 12, and 13 in the Ormrod (2011) text as references, as well as class discussions and presentations; the handout titled "Acquiring Literacy Skills That Have a Purpose and Deal with Real-Life Experiences" (Newman, Copple, and Bredekamp, 1998); the children's book they used previously for their literacy connection project (another assignment during this course that required students to analyze a character from a children's book using one of the developmental models we are studying); and the "Learning Literacy through Meaning" video available on our course webpage link and at the Annenberg Learner website.

Products/Representations of Learning
Each student or student pair will be asked to prepare one lesson activity that would take approximately twenty to thirty minutes to deliver to a class of elementary school third graders. The lesson activity will

- Select a character in a children's book and find evidence in the story of three distinctions of the self that were discussed in class: self-concept, self-esteem, and self-efficacy.
- Assist the third grader in developing at least one attribute in each of the three developmental domains—socioemotional, physical, and cognitive development—from early childhood to late adolescence and early adulthood.
- Develop these literacy skills: phonemic awareness, phonological awareness, and semantic cues.
- Provide quality suitable for inclusion in professional teaching portfolios.

Analysis of Lesson
This lesson produced numerous outstanding lesson plans by preservice teachers who went on to become certified as early childhood, middle school, and special education teachers. Students wrote lesson plans based on children's book characters that achieved the objectives to impart numerous *iSelf* attributions to their public school students. Many used their lesson plans proudly, as exemplary work in their professional portfolios.

High-Impact Practice: Enhancing Human Development Courses with the *iSelf* Model

Lesson Activity: "Autobiography and Human Development"

Coauthor Henry developed this lesson activity for his students at Clarion University.

This activity was used in Educational Psychology and Human Development and Learning courses.

Lesson Goals

The goal of this activity is to introduce the central issues in human development during early childhood, middle childhood, and adolescence. Students will develop an experiential understanding of the three major developmental stages of the children they will be teaching. Students will learn key terms or concepts in human development: universality and diversity; qualitative and quantitative changes. They will also learn the *Integrated Self* (*iSelf*) attributions and how to impart them in their elementary school classrooms.

Resources

Students will be asked to refer to the overhead presented in class titled "Central Issues" (which represents significant developmental milestones) (McDevitt & Ormrod, 2007, pp. 18–26). Students should draw upon their life experiences, as well as the three types or dimensions of development occurring in each stage: cognitive, physical, and socioemotional development. Students will also be provided the list of *iSelf* attributions.

Products/Representations of Learning

- Students will prepare short three- to five-minute presentations representing who they were in each of the three developmental stages in their lives.
- Students will draw a chart/diagram of what was developmentally unique about them (diversity), and experienced by most or all (universality). Students may reference the diagrams in the McDevitt & Ormrod text (2007, pp. 23–25).

In pairs, students will share their autobiography with each other. Students should work to make their communication and learning meaningful by fully describing those central issues that were experienced in each of the three developmental stages, and be prepared to discuss both unique and universal developmental attributes.

Activity Procedures
Students will
1. Form pairs at the beginning of class (5–10 minutes).
2. Listen and take notes during the instructor's presentation (15–20 minutes).
3. Read/review the Ormrod text, pp. 18–35, for ideas to use when developing their chart/diagrams (15–20 minutes).
4. Share their autobiographies in pairs (10–15 minutes).
5. Present their autobiographies in front of classmates/friends. (This activity takes the remainder of class and will be continued next class period until complete.)

Homework
Students will continue to work on constructing their charts/diagrams to make them more accurate, complete and comprehensive. Students' chart/diagrams will be turned in to the instructor at the end of class on Wednesday, and it will be graded.

List of **iSelf** *Attributions to Include in*
Each of the Three Developmental Stages
Self-concept, self-esteem, beliefs, morality, identity (four stages), purpose in life, hopes and dreams, self-efficacy, happiness, self-understanding, belonging, achievement, metacognition, emotional intelligence, self-affect, among others.

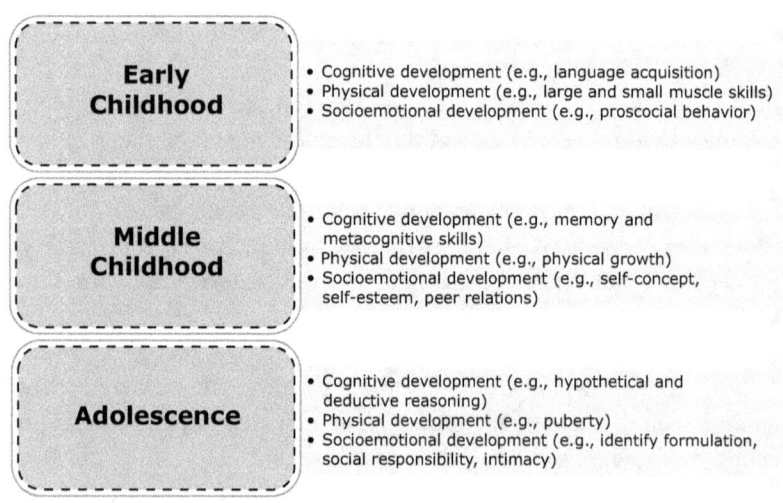

Figure 6. Three Stages of Development Diagram Used in Lesson Activity

Analysis of Lesson
This lesson activity can be used in courses in many subjects as a template to build self-knowledge. Students were very actively engaged in this activity because it required that they reflect upon who they are, and then integrate that self-knowledge into the academic subject.

Academic Advising

"Academic advising is one of the most important functions for success, especially for undecided students" (Tinto, 2004). Academic advisors guide students in navigating the complexities of higher education. Advisors "foster individual potential" and "help students develop and reinforce realistic self-perceptions and help them use this information in mapping out their futures" (NACADA, 2005). Finally, in keeping with our student success model, "Advisors encourage self-reliance and support students as they strive to make informed and responsible decisions, set realistic goals, and develop lifelong learning and self-management skills" (NACADA, 2005). There is a growing awareness that academic advisors need to take more of a whole person perspective when working with their advisees.

Based on the NACADA 2011 National Survey of Academic Advising (Carlstrom, 2013), "the median case load of advisees per full-time professional academic advisor is 296, or a ratio of 296 students to one full-time advisor. By institutional size, the median individual advisor caseloads are 233, 333, and 600 advisees for small, medium, and large institutions, respectively. The data show that the median numbers of advisees per advisor by institutional type are as follow: 441, 2-year; 260, public bachelor; 100, private bachelor; 300, public master; 179, private master; 285, public doctorate; 200, private doctorate; and 225, proprietary institutions."

Currently most academic advisors, CAPS professionals, career counselors, and even faculty are measured by number of advisee sessions, students seen in counseling sessions, or career counselor visits. Higher education institutions cannot realize their strategic visions or develop the whole person by adhering to these types of metrics.

Advisor ratios at many colleges and universities are far from being conducive to the formation of a personal relationship between student and advisor, which is the foundation for effective developmental advising. "As Winston (1994) notes, unfortunately, on many campuses today (especially at public four-year institutions) advising centers have student-advisor ratios in the hundreds and these ratios are growing. With such workloads, developmental advising is impossible, no matter what the philosophy or skills of the advisors" (Cuseo, 2008).

With these caseloads, it is difficult to require academic advisors to be the point persons for a full set of holistic student needs—personal, career, and academic. Our research demonstrates that shifting responsibilities from the professional academic advisor to the student is the most effective manner in which to fulfill professional responsibilities while supporting students fully and to the level of their expectations.

This shift can be accomplished successfully by conducting short workshops during first-year or orientation sessions. Faculty advisors can also hold short sessions to introduce *iSelf* distinctions and administer the *Success Predictor* in a team teaching format with career counselors, CAPS professionals, and/or academic advisors. Advising, whether delivered from a professional academic advisor or faculty member, is becoming more of a coaching role to create more self-directed students.

Advisors using the coaching model address numerous student needs and provide multiple entry points to student success through the creation of programs and services. Academic advisors have the unique opportunity to teach students how to take personal responsibility for their own lives—academic program selection, career choices, and well-being. The coaching method is suited to shifting the responsibility for success from the institutional functions to the student. Students will be better equipped to self-author their personal college career success pathways. Colleges and universities that teach self-authorship help ensure that students are actively engaged in their academic learning careers and take ownership of their decision-making and success pathways.

Once the *iSelf* and *Success Predictor* practices are introduced to students, they will be more self-directed and intrinsically motivated to author their own college learning experiences and pathways to achieve these.

Once students can assess themselves, they can more independently develop their own pathways to well-being and success. Academic advisors can use powerful assessment instruments such as Myers-Briggs Personality Profiling, the Devereux Student Strengths Assessment Mini-Form, Rosenburg's Self-Esteem Scale, and Ryff's Psychological Well-Being Scales. Advisors should also use the *iSelf* model to enable students to track their own development in each of the self-system and positive psychology attributions.

Promising Practice: Workshop Series on Student Success Dimensions

The Newnan Academic Advising Center at the University of Michigan offers workshops that focus on health and wellness, motivation, stress and anxiety, well-being and happiness (University of Michigan, 2016).

Additionally, this center offers workshops on how students can craft their degree, empowering a self-directed approach to creating their own student success pathways.

The University of Michigan is providing innovative leadership when integrating learning across fourteen units for what they call "engaged learning partnerships." Here they are making discoveries and connections during internships and service learning projects, and then relating these experiences to the concepts learned in the classroom. These students are documenting the self with the use of ePortfolios to collect artifacts of their experiences. The *iSelf* distinctions would further enhance this process as a nexus or lens for students, faculty, and internship coordinators to view the quality of the experience.

Dr. Malinda M. Matney, Senior Research Associate for Student Life, underscores the importance of helping students understand who they are, what they are learning, and professional competencies gained from their learning careers: "With the integrative learning, what we are discovering is that students are better able articulate their learning to parents, each other, future employers and future grad schools." She also advocates for the use of ePortfolios, which tend to be more common in academic departments, to capture artifacts that facilitate self-reflection while demonstrating personal and professional competencies. This is consistent with our view and that of the Carnegie Foundation: "More explicit rubrics for self-assessment, sometimes connected with portfolio development, may also serve powerful integrative purposes by making students more self-aware, self-directed learners" (Taylor, Huber, and Hutchings, 2004, p. 19).

The University of Michigan has found that by placing the student at the center of their curricula and co-curricular learning, they are better able to establish self-authorship, navigating conflict, creating one's own learning, and identifying and understanding multiple perspectives.

In particular, and aligned with these essential learning outcomes, they are interested in measuring whether students understand and can direct themselves as learners to recognize personal strengths and challenges and identify passions, interests, and sources of individual influences. They want students to be able to identify personal values and beliefs and a sense of purpose and how these inform creating learning and professional goals. These are clearly examples of placing the self of the students at the center of their own learning experiences.

Promising Practice: Individualized Student Learning Plans

An effective individualized student learning plan (ISLP) includes these elements in a template, easily visited and revisited throughout the student's college learning career:

- Student and contact information
- Name and contact information for the student's primary mentor/coach/advisor/faculty
- Information on other related existing educational plans such as 504 plans
- Key people on the student's ISLP team: career services, academic advising, health and well-being coaches, academic enrichment, psychological services, community engagement contacts, among others
- Entries by student success service providers with descriptions and date of comments
- Ties to the traditional academic information systems, such as transcripts and course schedules
- A place for the student to blog, to upload essays, videos, and make observations on how and when they learned *iSelf* distinctions for enhanced self-knowledge
- A place to record and describe observations about changing student behaviors, attributions such as discovering a new purpose in life, or expanded dreams
- A place for *Success Predictor* results, including the final workbook of dreams
- Descriptions of interests, dreams, and life experiences
- Plans with measurable goals for student's personal life, academics, and career, along with details on goal next steps and benchmarks or milestones
- Pathways to the college listing of experiential learning opportunities such as internships and engaged scholarship opportunities
- Records of competencies gained in and beyond the classroom (e.g., from leadership and teamwork, to writing and coding, and potentially earning badges)

This one-stop picture of the student's life helps create a whole person who is self-aware and supported. As academic advisors take on potentially more and more of the lead when supporting or coaching students they will have a tool to support their efforts. Further, students themselves will have a tool for self-authorship.

We envision that in the future, life coaches and student success coaches will develop and administer individualized student learning plans (ISLP), which could be labeled as *iPlans*, using a website such as MyEdu (https://www.myedu.com). The ISLP will be required for entering freshman at their orientation and first-year transition programs.

MyEdu is an online portal that helps students design their own student success plans. It was recently purchased by Blackboard (a course management system), so therefore these two essential services work together.

MyEdu has three component parts of student success:

- Personal profile—Interests, qualities, academic major, career pursuits, life stories, others
- Academic schedule—Integration with course catalogs and registrar's database; opportunities to choose the best course schedule based on work schedule, personal life, preferences, others.
- Internships and work—Using a national database of companies offering paid or nonpaid internships that could enhance resumes and professional competencies.

Students complete their own ISLP and maintain it over the four-year period. Using this tool allows students to take control of their own personalized learning program.

Promising Practice: Online Assessments

There are several online assessment tools to help students navigate their college learning careers, keeping track of both cognitive and noncognitive factors and measures. These tools can also be used by student success professionals to guide students more thoroughly.

Smarter Measure, a third-party service provider to colleges and universities, offers an online assessment tool that includes important noncognitive factors in its analysis of student readiness and persistence, attributes the *iSelf* model identifies as locus of control.

We see the growing use of electronic portfolios as an opportunity to keep track of and provide evidence for the development of both cognitive and noncognitive factors throughout students' learning careers.

Electronic Portfolios

ePortfolios document what students are learning about themselves and what is important to them. They are also used to support self-reflection to determine which experiences had personal meaning, and capture numerous accomplishments that demonstrate competencies.

Students use ePortfolios to collect their work, reflect upon strengths and weaknesses, and strive to improve. Equally beneficial are the data that advisors, counselors, faculty, departments, and institutions derive when they assess the work in portfolios, reflect upon it in curricular contexts, and use the data and reflections to plan for improvement. ePortfolios provide a rich resource for both students and student success professionals to learn about achieving important outcomes over time, make connections among disparate parts of the curriculum, gain insights leading to improvement, and develop identities as learners or as facilitators of learning.

Further, ePortfolios capture important evidence of personal and professional growth that can be used as a part of a future job application.

Career Counseling

We are encouraged by the growing number of courses and workshops that are being offered to college students that integrate two and often three student success functions that help focus career decision through the integration of self-discovery, academic program selection and internships, or real-world learning opportunities.

We think it is remarkable that today's college students hunger for self-knowledge and knowing what makes them unique. Students thrive in courses where they are encouraged to take a life-span approach to envisioning their lives.

We have also found that a course or workshop designed with a bold vision for societal change actually empowers and motivates students to take leadership roles to impact the world while in college and then in their lives.

Promising Practice: Integrating Career and Academic Advising

St. Petersburg College in Florida describes its integrated approach to student success:

> Integrated Career and Academic Advising: We know that students are more successful if they have a distinct academic or career goal in mind. We concentrate on helping students identify career choices as early as possible so they can follow the proper academic paths to reach their goals. Advisors reach out

to students individually and in classroom visits to help them explore options with career aptitude tools. Highlighting the institutional focus upon the student, making the student centered experience real, *SPC* career specialists, advisors, counselors and faculty members will assist our students in mapping out their individualized student learning plan's (ISLP) on a semester-by-semester basis. (St. Petersburg, 2016, p. 1)

As we noted in Chapter 3, St. Petersburg College's mission promotes student success through "education, career development and self-discovery." The college ensures this mission is met in tangible ways by using proactive, integrated outreach to help students identify career choices and develop supportive ISLPS to guide their academic achievements.

Promising Practice: Designing Your Life Course

At Stanford University, 17 percent of seniors enroll in "Designing Your Life," a course for juniors and seniors to learn about who they are and how this self-knowledge impacts their career and life-course trajectories.

The course's lessons give students the perspectives they need to navigate decisions about life and work postgraduation. Students explore gratitude, generosity, self-awareness, and adaptability, among numerous distinctions that map to the *iSelf* distinctions. Paraphrasing the Stanford website, the course includes seminar-style discussions, role-playing, short writing assignments, guest speakers, and individual mentoring and coaching. Small group dialogue is held in regular section groups that form during the first week and meet during class time. The capstone assignment is the creation of an "Odyssey Years Plan" focusing on taking action in the 3–5 years following Stanford graduation. Alumni say they still refer back to their odyssey plans and revise them as their lives and careers progress.

The goal of "Designing Your Life" is to change higher education by transforming each student into a person who will go out into the world, effect change, and be a leader. Students learn their life purpose, perhaps the most important *iSelf* attribute to learn in life.

Stanford recently developed a pared-down version of "Designing Your Life" for freshmen and sophomores as a complement to their academic advising. This additional program, "Designing Your Stanford," provides a great example of integrating personal, academic, and career counseling dimensions, as we propose in our *iSuccess* student success model (Stanford, 2016).

High-Impact Practice: Aligning Life Purpose and Career Using the *Success Predictor*

The *Success Predictor* assessment instrument was administered in a short workshop format by co-coauthor Henry to both first-year and second-year students.

The Center for the Self in Schools offered a short, one-day, three session workshop to help students understand their life purpose and dreams, then choose their academic program based upon those dreams, and then select a potential career path and internships that would manifest such expressions of themselves.

The result? Students took it upon themselves to take ownership of their well-being and future directions.

For example, one student who had limited financial means to even attend college expressed an interest in a "practical" career to satisfy her parents' demands. As such, she was just going through the motions of attending classes and was not emotionally engaged in her expensive education. Through the workshop, she transformed her understanding of who she was and what she was meant to do with her life—the distinct difference she could make.

She changed her academic major from Spanish to Social Policy and International Relations, and she then actively found and accepted an internship in Peru. She went on to empower inner-city people to make their communities and neighborhoods safer and cleaner and to improve their personal health by reducing obesity rates. Her self-esteem and confidence soared, giving rise to a dynamic personality that had lain dormant.

High-Impact Practice: Summer Bridge Program Using the *iSelf* Model

Coauthor Henry, through The Brzycki Group, conducts summer bridge programs for students planning to go to college, whether undecided or firm in their college choices. The program combines personal counseling (self-understanding and esteem) with academic advising (which college academic program to enter), with career counseling (which profession), and student engagement (how to make learning real world). One participant, "Ryan," was diagnosed with numerous learning disabilities that severely impacted his high school academic career, and he barely graduated. By summer, he had not yet even applied to colleges.

Further, he suffered from a severe poor self-image because during his freshman year in high school, given his academic difficulties, his mother decided that Ryan must be hard of hearing, which his doctors determined was not true. She found a hearing device that was worn around his neck and hung down to his chest, with an earpiece going into both ears. This seems archaic, and was. Ryan had to wear this around all through high school and was the brunt of jokes and bullying, degrading his sense of self-worth.

Ryan's parents were high power, successful professionally, and believed—were determined—that their son was going to be successful as well. They had placed so much pressure on him to achieve academically that he literally cried every evening when attempting to do his homework.

Through appreciative inquiry about his strengths, his talents, and his dreams for his life, we discovered that he was very gifted in anything to do with the sea, sailing, navigating using charts and radar, fishing, lobstering, fixing boat motors and carpentry, among others. His self-esteem soared upon learning that he was actually gifted and that these could help him realize a dream, to develop fish farms off the coast of Maine. Further, he gained the understanding that he could determine his future, his own pathway to manifesting his dream. (He deepened his experience of two *iSelf* distinctions, self-determination and locus of control.) He applied and was accepted to the Maine Maritime Academy, which has rolling admissions and an active learning support program.

Through internships, service learning opportunities at his college, along with additional summer jobs and projects, he strengthened his newfound self-esteem through achievement, and he saw the results that he produced in the world. He built boats, fixed boat motors, offered guided tours, and did hands-on internships where he could gain self-efficacy, the belief that he could attain his goals.

Ryan also learned that being a sensitive soul, having a caring heart, and wanting to help humanity by feeding them and making them safer were all good qualities beyond his academic course work. He was a whole person!

He had hopes and dreams that had laid dormant, unconscious to even him, and he became a new person.

He became cognitively (*iSelf* attribution of metacognition) aware that he indeed had these learning disabilities, and took action (*iSelf* attribution of self-determination) to obtain the appropriate study skills and organization assistance that he needed. He no longer felt as though he needed to hide his imperfections. Further, he was no longer emotionally upset about not being able to handle the increased academic requirements—evidence of increased emotional intelligence and management. He could also feel genuine happiness for who he is (*iSelf* attributions of emotional intelligence, self-affect, and happiness).

Ryan went on to major in marine sciences and start his own boating and fishing business in Maine, satisfying his own vision of success in his life.

High-Impact Practice: Integrating Career Counseling and Internships Using the *iSuccess* Model

Internships become powerful real-world learning experiences when they reveal potential career paths that align with the self-knowledge students gain through their internships. University professionals coordinating, overseeing, or mentoring interns need training in a comprehensive framework that intentionally produces growth in the attributes of the *iSelf* model. Coauthor Elaine served as an internship mentor at WPSU Penn State, and she incorporated career counseling through the use of one-one-one interactions using affirmative inquiry with Myers-Briggs personality profile analysis to assist a student, "Leah," with her identity, motivation, and self-concept.

Leah's formal internship review (reproduced with permission) indicates she reflected deeply on her experience and gained an enhanced sense of several *iSelf* attributes, including personal locus of control and purpose:

> This entire semester has given me the tools, education, and guidance I needed to make decisions for my senior year. I owe most of this to my mentor, Elaine Brzycki. She took the time to meet with me for about an hour every Monday to critically look at the work I did, give me feedback, provide career advice, and help me realize my potential. I am much less anxious about senior year, and I believe I possess the education necessary to join the workforce. I now have the knowledge and experience I need to be confident for the future and after graduation. Each day I came to intern I left motivated, inspired, and optimistic. Every day was a new learning opportunity. I absorbed so much here that couldn't be replicated in a classroom. Receiving genuine, helpful, personal advice is something that most students cannot get on a regular basis. I am so thankful that I had such a great mentor during this transitional period in my life, I believe that this is the semester (junior year, spring semester) that college students require the most guidance, and I am very lucky I found such a motivating, positive experience.
>
> Through this internship I learned so much about my personal motivations and myself. I often wondered why I never felt satisfied with the jobs, classes, relationships, or experiences that others did and why I choose to intern at a public broadcasting station instead of the big entertainment media internships my peers raved about. I found this is because I am a mission oriented individual; the only way for me to feel truly happy at the job is if I support the cause behind it. This is why I was drawn to WPSU and their mission to support lifelong learning. While interning here, I fell in love with PBS, the mission, the atmosphere, the day-to-day work, and the creativity behind each project. If I get the opportunity to fulfill my career aspirations and become a

producer, I believe I will be lead a rewarding and happy life. . . . For most of my college career I have felt guilty for pursuing a Bachelor of the Arts degree through the College of Communications because my mom, dad, twin sister, and brother are chemists, scientists, and chemical engineers. This pressure to pursue a STEM degree along with my family making snide comments about my choice to pursue a career in humanities and media made me feel very insecure for a few years. This internship is the reason I no longer feel like a disappointment for my choice. I think that there are multiple ways to make an impact in the world. For example, whether you are purifying drinking water for people in need or whether you are the one raising awareness that the effort needs help, you are both contributing equally important aspects. We need all types of thinkers, workers, and educators in the world; this is what makes it such a dynamic and interesting place.

This internship has been quite enlightening. It is eye opening to see the possibilities at your fingertips once you realize your personal strengths and motivations.

Along with public broadcasting, I believe that I could have some new potential career paths that Elaine helped me realize—mainly counseling, advising, and grant writing. It is comforting to know that I have other options if something were to not work out. She also suggested I look into graduate school, something I have never considered before. I think it could be life changing, I am now considering going and have done some research on the subject.

University personnel offering internships should encourage these moments that impact the lives of interns. Leah came to the internship having made her own choices, and she was self-motivated and took responsibility for her future. But she benefited greatly from a mentor seeing and acknowledging her strengths, a mentor who incorporated knowledge of career counseling practices into job assignment oversight. Because Leah's confidence and hopes for the future soared, her overall well-being did as well.

College students want a model or framework to understand who they are and what they could be doing with their lives. The *Success Predictor* along with the *iSelf* model are very effective tools to assist career counselors integrate the personal with the professional, making certain to take into consideration the whole person they work with. Short-term workshops like those provided at Stanford University, Clarion University, and The Brzycki Group, and internships like those offered by Penn State and St. Petersburg College, make for ideal student-centered learning platforms. These workshops and internships should be intentionally designed to produce *iSelf* model attributions if counselors want to ensure that students' expectations are being met for value of their college training.

Counseling and Psychological Services (CAPS)

With the increased focus upon developing the whole person across numerous university functions, CAPS can help integrate a full array of preventative well-being strategies university-wide.

Promising Practice: Focus on Life Purpose

Harvard University announced in March 2016 the hiring of a new position whose job is to teach students about the meaning and purpose of their lives. This is an example of dedicating scarce resources toward the inner life of students versus adding more and more external supports. Harvard's "attempt to enhance the experience of students by working . . . on ways to foster personal growth during their four years as undergraduates" complements the *iSuccess* model's high-impact practices. Helping students find purpose in life (one of the *iSelf* attributions) can transform students and their college experiences and address the holistic needs of students throughout their entire college learning career. Katherine Steele, project manager for freshman programming, indicated, "Seniors said they learned a lot from chemistry and history and whatnot, but never really learned how to live life" as one justification for the new programming. This is 21st-century student success in action (Silvergate, 2016).

Promising Practice: Life Coaching and Student Success Coaching

Florida State University (FSU), a large Research I university, uses life coaches in a partnership between

> the Center for Academic Retention and Enhancement (CARE) and the Advising First Center for College Life Coaching. Through College Life Coaching, FSU provides additional support through a structured program designed to increase students' effectiveness in and out of the classroom. As part of the effort, the CARE partnership contributes to the successful retention and graduation of undergraduate students. Participating students receive one-on-one personal coaching to assist them in continuing their successful engagement with the FSU campus, as well as effective transition into the upper division and their respective major program of study. The coaches work closely with academic advisors, CARE staff, and other campus resources to support CARE students in achieving their academic and personal goals. Students who receive coaching typically reach their goals faster, enjoy college

more, have higher grade point averages, and have higher rates of retention. (Florida State University, 2016)

Life coaches could eventually replace academic advisors and career counselors and be known as the primary contact for all dimensions of the student experience. Life coaches will need skills in advising, personal counseling, and assessments, as examples. Many professionals in academic advising already address career counseling needs and vice versa.

High Point University, a private comprehensive institution rooted in the liberal arts, offers a future looking model of student success to which the university has committed interdisciplinary resources. Every High Point University freshman is assigned a Success Coach (which is often synonymous with life coaching) to assist during the first year of college, which then continues through graduation.

Success Coaches are responsible for providing appropriate academic and transitional support to first-year students applicable to all aspects of the student's life tasks: academic, personal, social, and career. First, coaches assist students in making a successful transition to college life. Then, through close one-on-one relationships, coaches help motivate students and help them find their dreams and passions in life. Finally, coaches help students develop academic plans and identify experiences that will help manifest this sense of purpose and passion. This model and use of life coaching is exemplary in our view.

In this following student testimonial, we see the qualities of the Success Coach, who does life coaching with kindness and passion, placing the student's need first:"My Coach was the best Success Coach I could have asked to have by my side during my freshman year. She was not only helpful, but she was also kind, considerate, flexible, understanding and, overall, very supportive throughout my whole academic career! She has a true passion for her job and for the students that she works with, I am very thankful for her."

Associate Dean of Student Success Dr. Beth Holder is providing visionary leadership to not only High Point University but also higher education, by demonstrating that a student-centered, holistic student success model works for both the student and the institution.

Promising Practice: Online Therapy

Therapy Assisted Online (TAO) is an online program used to treat student anxiety at the University of Florida. Here are some facts about TAO:

1. TAO is a seven-week, interactive, web-based program that provides assistance to help students overcome anxiety.
2. It is based on well-researched and highly effective strategies for helping anxiety.
3. Over the course of the seven weeks, participants watch videos, complete exercises, and meet with a counselor via video conferencing for a 10–15 minute consultation.
4. Weekly exercises take approximately 30–40 minutes to complete.

We have found comprehensive research is being conducted by departments within university student success functions to demonstrate the effectiveness of their practices. For example, during the fall 2013 semester, the University of Florida compared outcomes for individual face-to-face psychotherapy, group psychotherapy, and TAO for students with anxiety across seven sessions. Results from the university's pilot study indicated that TAO participants' symptoms were reduced and functioning was increased at or above the level of participants in traditional counseling services.

The University of Florida's Counseling and Wellness Center is providing visionary leadership by experimenting with new ideas (http://www.counseling.ufl.edu/cwc/tao) that are producing important wellness results.

Promising Practice: Student Wellness across the University

The Ohio State University, through its Office of Student Life, is implementing a framework that extends and integrates personal wellness into career services, academic advising, and student engagement, among some thirty university units and departments. The mission of student affairs and student life is "to create an extraordinary student experience," clearly attempting to provide transformational opportunities.

In our view this is a promising practice because Ohio State is integrating student affairs with academic affairs, while placing students' well-being at the center of their college learning careers. They see the complex interactions among all wellness dimensions as key components to student success: "career, creative, emotional, environmental, financial, intellectual, physical, social and spiritual." Further, they see addressing the needs of the whole person as critical to student success in college and beyond. Ohio State understands that well-being requires an integrated view.

If colleges and universities provide these resources to students, they will utilize them, because it is in their self-interest to do so. They will have more of what they want from college—training for a successful life.

High-Impact Practice: Well-Being Workshops Using the *iSelf* Model

The Center for the Self in Schools designed a workshop using the *iSelf* model as the framework for well-being, where a number of key distinctions were discussed.

Purpose in life: Why do you think you are here at this time in human history? What is your unique purpose in life? What have you experienced in your life thus far that compels you to take action to impact a quality or issue?

One student indicated that she had been sexually abused as a child. She went home and communicated with her mother how she had come to understand that this experience in her life, trauma really, informed her unique purpose. The mother and daughter worked on their purposes in life together and then took actions to manifest these. The mother communicated for the first time that she too was abused as a child. As both were sexually abused as children by family members, and so, armed with new self-understanding and purpose in life, they went on to develop a sexual-abuse prevention program that was eventually proposed for statewide adoption.

The mother, who was diagnosed with bipolar affective disorder, with the approval of her medical doctor, reduced her medications after reshaping her entire paradigm of self and her reality and becoming whole again with herself, which created a healthy balance in her brain chemistry.

The girl, with the genetic factor associated with bipolar affective disorder, could have easily fallen into this family diagnosis, instead of gaining a new level of emotional intelligence through her learning. Her learning took the form of writing in journals and poems, diagnosing these from a self-lens, and subsequent short meetings to discuss purpose in life and motivations to take action, demonstrating the effectiveness of using *iSelf* distinctions when learning about how personal knowledge impacts well-being, resulting in enhanced personal well-being.

Through our work together, we would have seen changes in the brain gray matter of both the mother and the daughter, both in the prefrontal cortex (where, psychologically, executive functioning resides) and in the left amygdala (the brain's emotional center). Therefore, the daughter prevented affective disorders through learning about herself and becoming more emotionally connected, passionate really, about her purpose in life. Many disorders that are often treated with psychotropic medications can be treated through changes in the brain chemistry and functioning, and learning about one's higher purpose in life can literally change brain functioning by forming healthy new connections between executive functioning and emotional responses.

We, along with numerous colleagues, have found that emotional well-being can be achieved if any individual—child, adolescent or adult—is taught that he has a unique self with specific attributions such as unique purpose. This alone shifts his way of being to more of an ontological inquiry, with a newfound inner peace, and leads to subsequent changes in behavior and experiences of emotional well-being characterized as less anxiety and stress.

Student Engagement

Student engagement covers a wide range of related activities from student scholarship, to global experiences, to internships. Colleges and universities employ a range of terminology to describe student engagement, such as civic engagement, community engagement, community-based learning, experiential learning, real-world learning, and service learning. When institutions refer to engaged scholarship, they usually speak of curricular, classroom-based, and research activities. When they refer to student engagement, this encompasses a broader array of activities both curricular and co-curricular. Universities provide online portals into identifying and applying for these experiences, but many are promoted only within specific academic departments for their own students, rather than university-wide.

Promising Practice: Community Engagement

St. Petersburg College, through the SPC Center of Excellence, enables students to go out into the community to work with Pinellas County elementary, middle school, and high school students to help them succeed in school and have healthy self-esteem (thereby imparting a key *iSelf* model attribution, self-esteem, to local school children).

At Clarion University in an educational psychology course that coauthor Henry taught, students designed skits about different types of bullying behavior and how to intervene and even prevent these. They took their class work into a local public middle school to both rave reviews and impactful results in terms of the decline of future incidences.

Promising Practice: The Engaged University

In 2014, Cornell University launched a new initiative, Engaged Cornell, to create a new model and direction for higher education, one in which public engagement is deeply ingrained, fully institutionalized, and effectively taught and implemented. Through this initiative, students graduating from Cornell will enter the world as educated global citizens who practice respect and empathy; seek collaboration, cooperation, and creativity; embrace differences and diversity in all aspects of their personal, professional, and civic lives; and are dedicated to working together to help solve some of the world's most intractable problems (Cornell Chronicle, 2014). Some universities integrate student engagement throughout the campus, where it becomes the cultural norm.

At the Florida State University (FSU), student engagement is a strategic goal with these priorities:

- Develop strategies to increase student engagement, promote learning opportunities, and foster inclusiveness across campus.
- Enhance and support student leadership learning initiatives.
- Expand internship and experiential opportunities.
- Expand internationalization efforts in partnership with Academic Affairs.
- Increase mental health and wellness resources.
- Implement Division of Student Affairs student leader learning outcomes assessment.
- Encourage the study of the college student experience and program effectiveness to promote student success.

Through a student engagement focus, FSU demonstrates university-wide integration of resources for mental health and wellness, faculty teaching to increase new learning opportunities both inside and outside of the university, and internships to help students develop career competencies such as leadership skills.

FSU offers students a matrix that details real-world learning activities such as internships and project-based learning activities such as service learning. The matrix includes student-faculty scholarship opportunities in all academic courses. A student wanting to build competencies, personal or professional, can choose to enroll into a course based on the type of engagement and relevancy to the student's personal or professional development needs. Students can update their individualized-personalized learning plan and portfolio for their academic advisors to see, along with future employers.

FSU's "enriching communities" can be mapped to student engagement opportunities to make learning real world. "Through education" means that projects assigned in class, service learning and internships map to classroom assignments and course objectives. Faculty design courses with assignments that involve the wider community and address local and societal problems for "career development and self-discovery."

Additionally, we would underscore the need to develop within FSU's matrix deeper and more refined distinctions about self that can be mapped to the *iSelf* distinctions to illuminate self-knowledge attributions such as emotional intelligence, purpose and dreams, locus of control, identity formulation, among numerous others that are so critical to shaping success pathways.

High-Impact Practice: Integrating Student Engagement through University Themes

When institutions define universal themes to impact society, as The Pennsylvania State University did recently, they create the opportunity to connect students to real-world learning opportunities that can actually make a difference. Students want to do meaningful work and connect with something larger than themselves.

Coauthor Elaine developed a high-impact project at the university that connected students to one of the university's critical institution-wide themes of sustaining natural resources. This cross-departmental project included internships and student engagement, faculty research, community partnerships and outreach, foundation and corporate funders, and public television distribution.

The core of the project was the WPSU produced and distributed *Water Blues, Green Solutions*, a national public broadcast documentary to educate communities on green storm water infrastructure. The documentary won a 2014 Mid-Atlantic Emmy Award, aired on PBS stations nationwide, and was distributed to every member of Congress. In collaboration with the project and the university's efforts in the science of science communication, faculty developed and delivered a research evaluation that measured the impact of the project's documentary and other media on public perception of watershed issues. Their work indicated that the project raised support for green policy solutions to water management in the Philadelphia area by more than 13 percent.

WPSU and one of the university's outreach units, Penn State Center–Pittsburgh, partnered on screening events to foster community discussion with government leaders about Pittsburgh's green solutions. The project also provided online toolkits with discussion questions, event format ideas, and suggestions for community collaborators to help facilitate event planning. Water organizations embedded the videos in their water curriculum. An online digital library continues to provide visitors with inspiration.

The student engagement component tied to filmmaking and hands-on community development. Communications students interned on the film in production and marketing. Students from the Landscape Architecture department participated in an activation event to revitalize community green infrastructure on Lancaster Avenue in Philadelphia. The students worked side by side with the Philadelphia Water Department, corporate volunteers from the Subaru Corporation, and environmental organizations to redevelop overgrown roadside bioswales. Penn State public relations personnel prepared a story on the event that was posted on the university's website as an example of student engagement. And students and faculty continue to use the online videos in landscape architecture classes (http://waterblues.org/explore/stories).

Water Blues, Green Solutions demonstrated cross-departmental collaboration and student engagement with real-world challenges. The university gained national visibility for its strengths in sustainability. Moving forward, these high-impact projects have implications for the university's student engagement strategic priority, because they can help faculty and students make important community connections that make student engagement substantive, meaningful, and memorable.

To be effective, a single unit within the university needs to take ownership and provide leadership for these high-impact projects tied to universal themes. In this case, WPSU had previously produced national documentaries and developed community outreach activities, so WPSU had the background to serve as the lead. Not every institution has the good fortune to have ties into the community through public broadcasting, and not every institution has outreach or extension divisions with natural ties to external partners. But every college and university has community relationships upon which to build, and the capacity to integrate plans around university themes.

Engagement Project Elements
The *Water Blues, Green Solutions* high-impact media project connected to a university theme, and it engaged students in making a difference locally and national. Here is a list of project elements:

Media
- Award-winning videos and documentaries
- Interactive videos, graphics, and other media for the web
- K-16 learning materials
- Community toolkits
- PBS broadcast and web distribution
- Topics—Water, environment, well-being, health, energy

Faculty
- Research evaluation of media impact
- Peer-reviewed publication of research

- Content experts on media advisory board
- Project advisors
- Ties to science-of-science communication efforts
- Cross-unit collaborations

Student Engagement
- Service learning at community events
- Real-world learning for media interns and graduate assistants
- Enhanced materials for traditional and online classes

Outreach
- Partnerships with national organizations
- Cultivation of private foundations and corporations
- Community engagement
- Social media
- Press exposure
- Conferences—National and international
- Distribution to US Congress

Integration through Technology

Through technology, colleges and universities can offer institution-wide integration of services, if all the functional areas plan in advance and agree on the centrality of self-knowledge, wellness, and self-determined measures of success.

Therefore, technology will be critical to advancing the *iSuccess* model. Technology can enhance student well-being and self-knowledge by providing, for example,

- Confidential, accessible, nonjudgmental mental health services and well-being assessments, in which students can reflect on their growth in each of the *iSelf* distinctions and faculty can tie assignments to this reflection and growth.
- Student access to the *Success Predictor*, as a part of freshman orientation, and then throughout students' four years to see how their hopes and dreams have been changed or heightened by their college experiences.

Technology can also help institutions integrate the five student success functions by providing the following:

- Documentation and recognition, both institutional and student self-reported, of noncognitive strengths gained beyond academic grades, through internships and engaged scholarship experiences.
- Records of professional competencies gained through student engagement experiences such as leadership and team-building.
- Centralized portals of student engagement opportunities offering clear links and simple navigation between departments and functions. For instance, some institutions offer a database allowing students to narrow results based on their interests.
- Videos and other multimedia that help promote and make visible the value to students of the institution's integrated efforts.

There are several advantages to increasing the use of technology when delivering student success programs. Technology can help

1. Increase access by more students given the bottleneck in service availability in key university functional areas or departments (e.g., CAPS).
2. Reduce the cost of providing one-on-one service, permitting highly trained professionals to dedicate more of their efforts and talents toward more holistic coaching.
3. Engage millennials and GenZ students who are technology centric in their views of the world, and hence extremely comfortable interacting with multimedia platforms to enhance their success through integrated learning applications.
4. Deliver on the promise of higher education to prepare young adults for a successful life
5. Assess student success beyond graduation rates

As a counterbalance to when technology can be isolating, the institution needs to continually reinforce its commitment to well-being and empower staff to reinforce the missing human-to-human interaction.

Final Thoughts

Many of the promising practices included in this chapter and throughout the book were discovered through our research, or were submitted as a result of answering our call for submissions in the ACPA March 3, 2016, *eCommunity* newsletter. All of the submitters realize that student success professionals need an interdisciplinary model and set of practices that cut across curricular and co-curricular learning, resulting in an integration of the whole person with learning. This is student-centered learning within higher education. Noncognitive factors, such as emotions, play a critical role in student success, in that a positive emotional approach facilitates a sense of well-being that, in turn, enhances a willingness to learn.

The *iSuccess* model builds upon student-centered well-being practices that, when used as the central organizing principle, help bring the various university student success functions together for an integrated student experience.

High-impact teaching practices creatively convey course content while simultaneously imparting numerous *iSelf* attributes, such as emotional intelligence, and the importance of a personal and professional identity.

We are all partners in a common cause of guiding adolescent students into young adulthood and then on to adulthood so they can thrive on their own, using the three high-impact student success practices discussed in this book: the *iSelf* model, *SAC*, and *Success Predictor*.

The idea of student success has grown over the past three to five years. At one time, it meant helping students go through successful onboarding experiences, helping them to choose an academic major and requisite courses, orienting them to campus resources, and hoping for the best. Often this meant a lonely existence for students, detached from their purpose in attending a rigorous (not to mention expensive) program. Frontline educators did not have metrics to measure the quality of students' experiences nor their learning outcomes. Today, it means helping students understand who they are and their unique, personal pathways to a positive learning career and broader college experience that prepares them for a positive life-course trajectory. As one student recently asserted, "I am here to learn about who I am!"

Academic advisors and student affairs counselors are often the first professional education experts with whom a new student has substantive contact, usually during an orientation event. Typical orientation events have included familiarizing students with the "ins and outs" of campus life, how to register for courses, what clubs and organizations are available, and campus and town maps and tours.

But now, there is a growing trend to include more in-depth analysis to help students navigate not only their college environment, but more importantly and relevant, their inner psychological states of awareness, such as personality profiles, academic and personal strengths, emotional well-being, mind-set, and spiritual growth.

This recent trend poses potential problems for traditional academic advisors in that they are not trained or prepared to expand their thinking and expertise to include these other student success dimensions. Often this leaves this academic-based group digging in deeper to establish their own boundaries, their lines of responsibility, sharply against those of other important student success functions (e.g., career counseling, student affairs personal coaching, among others).

Universities are making strides. There are examples of where student life outcomes take into consideration metrics that focus upon students' self-attributions. Students are assessed on the degree to which they understand and direct themselves as learners, or have self-direction in their learning careers. Students are being asked to recognize personal strengths and challenges, and to be able to identify their passions, purpose, interests, and topics of curiosity that influence their learning about life. Students are asked to articulate their personal values and beliefs and how these influence their learning and decisions in life.

As we've demonstrated in this chapter, some institutions are already exploring proven high-impact practices that effectively infuse well-being approaches beyond counseling and psychological services into academic advising, curricula, and career counseling. At Brown University, CAPS pursues knowledge and skills in cutting edge, evidence-based approaches that attend to the whole person; this is a passion of the institution that impacts all academic departments and divisions.

We close these final thoughts with one of our favorite examples of applying high-impact practices. At American Public University where coauthor Henry was both a dean and professor, we used the *Self Across the Curriculum* (*SAC*). We required all students at the beginning of every new sixteen-week course to discuss with their professor how the course could help them better understand their distinct purpose in life. Faculty members designed weekly lesson activities that assisted students in designing real-world projects that allowed them to work, for example, on ways to stop bullying in middle schools. Students became engaged in their learning by being intrinsically motivated to use their talents and skills to deal with real problems. Further, they encouraged and moved each other by revealing their highest hopes and dreams for a better world where children and people treated each other with kindness and love.

Retention rates increased by 26 percent for the entire School of Education, with student satisfaction scores going up by almost 40 percent, demonstrating that students felt empowered to persevere and were happier about who they are and their course work when they learned about themselves and saw the tangible contributions they could make.

FINAL THOUGHTS

Throughout our book, we demonstrated the centrality of well-being and self-knowledge to student success, and shared promising and high-impact practices as examples for institutions to use to strengthen their own student success mission.

We presented the *iSuccess* model and its three high-impact practices, which offer higher education a new lens through which to view students, representing a breakthrough prevention model and student success approach. This systemic model integrates student success functions across all levels of the institution to aid students in achieving their self-authored educational, career, and personal goals, empowering their higher purpose for a life of contribution.

Now, in these final thoughts, we summarize some of this book's tangible suggestions for actions that individuals, professionals, and institutions can take to advance student success, guided by the *iSuccess* model.

We then conclude with personal reflections that we hope will inspire action by each of our readers as they reflect upon their own pathways to manifest their unique purpose in life.

Suggestions for . . .

Students

Individual students and student groups do not need to wait for their college or university to make systemic changes in order to put well-being and self-knowledge at the center of their college learning experiences. Students can

- Read and learn more about the *iSelf* distinctions, and provide themselves with a new awareness of the self-system and positive psychology attributions that have been shown to lead to positive life trajectories.
- Complete the *Success Predictor* to proactively develop a structure to accomplish their goals and pursue their dreams in college and in life.

- Develop peer-to-peer counseling groups to discuss the *iSelf* distinctions, complete the *Success Predictor*, and encourage self-authorship.
- Reach out to faculty and student success professionals to engage in co-curricular, extracurricular, and community-based projects.
- Create groups to meet with university leaders and discuss needs and request resources to support their well-being.
- Continue to voice that the purpose of education is well-being for self, family, friends, institutions, and society.

Faculty

Faculty can strengthen their students' self-knowledge and well-being in both simple and complex ways. Faculty can

- Read the *iSelf* distinctions and incorporate at least one distinction into an assignment, noting for students when they have strengthened their awareness of the distinction. For example, self-efficacy can be demonstrated by defending a mathematical theorem, and locus of control can be demonstrated by designing a marketing campaign.
- Explore ways to incorporate emotional learning in cognitive assignments, such as connecting assignments to making a meaningful contribution to the community.
- Form a departmental group to explore ways to encourage and recognize students' self-knowledge and self-responsibility.
- Engage the faculty senate in discussing ways to improve policies for integration of *Self Across the Curriculum*.

Student Success Professionals

Academic, career, and counseling and psychological services (CAPS) advisors can make a significant difference by developing programs for students, working with each other across units, and reaching up through the hierarchies of leadership for institutional change. Academic, career, CAPS, and engagement professionals can

- Hold inter- and intraunit discussion groups on the promising and high-impact practices in this book to explore ones to incorporate into their functions and institutions.
- Develop preventative programming based on the *iSelf*'s self-system and positive psychology attributions.

- Create new student handbooks and other resources.
- Build the *Success Predictor* into first-year orientation programs.
- Develop four-year programs that support students' progress towards their personal and professional goals.
- Design metrics to measure students' well-being.
- Train faculty in the many ways to impart well-being and self-knowledge using the *iSuccess* model.
- Make presentations to the faculty senate and university leaders on the *iSelf* distinctions they feel are most important to include in the institution's mission and in interdepartmental programs.

Institutions of Higher Education

IHEs can work across units to initiate university-wide systems of support for student success. IHEs should bring together representatives from the five student success functions and other leaders to

- Develop a new mission statement that puts well-being at the center of the institution.
- Develop an institution-wide plan for tangible and integrated programs that deliver on the promise of the well-being mission.
- Determine institution-wide themes to engage students in making a difference in society.
- Design metrics to measure how the new well-being mission is helping to achieve institutional goals.
- Work with information technology professionals to develop online systems for students to self-manage their goals, competencies, and accomplishments.
- Redesign general education programs to include the values of well-being, self-knowledge, and societal contribution.

Professional Organizations

Professional organizations can work collectively to

- Develop professional standards that cut across all the functions; develop competencies and practices for a professional track called "student success professional."
- Sponsor research to collect examples, beyond those in this book, of promising practices at IHEs.

It is to the advantage of leaders of today's colleges and universities to be out in front of changing student needs. Many of those who supported this book by submitting their forward-thinking work realize that changes need to be made, and they are providing necessary leadership.

As we indicated earlier in the pages of this book, the advantages are many for IHEs who adopt the *iSuccess* model and include the following: (1) current students and alumni alike will be able to see the lifelong value they gained from their alma mater's emphasis on well-being and self-knowledge; (2) each of the student success functional units will see reduced costs of training on their particular area of expertise through a systemic and integrated approach; (3) each functional unit and all its professionals will have a common language to speak about students' needs and plan for the future; (4) student success professionals will have a set of high-impact student success practices, thereby increasing their effectiveness when supporting students; (5) more seamless collaboration among functions will ameliorate departmental battles for control and power; (6) happier, healthier, flourishing people.

Personal Reflections

As trustees of the human condition and providers of the pathway to the good life, let us, as higher education professionals, search for new ways to realize our highest visions for what is possible. We believe that it is indeed possible to do more and to help people take action to create a better society.

We can teach people how not to hate others who are different than ourselves. We can teach empathy, taking new perspectives on how to have a view of self and life that is inclusive and actually cares for others because of their differences, not in spite of them. We can teach how to handle the emotion of anger, with strategies to express it appropriately and more effectively. We can teach people a mind-set that allows for uncertainty, complexity, and how to process change effectively. We can take care of people preventatively, rather than reacting to crises. We can teach people how to connect with their innate goodness and contribute to a better society and life for all. We can make well-being our mission.

As we have demonstrated, the research is compelling and conclusive that poor self-knowledge is associated with a broad range of mental disorders and social problems, including depression, suicidal tendencies, eating disorders, anxiety, substance abuse, violence, and identity disorders. Self-knowledge is the number one protective factor for mental health. We can help frontline educators and mental health practitioners focus on teaching self-knowledge as the key to academic and career success and also as a mental illness prevention model. We believe that if an institution's focus is on student self-knowledge and well-being, then people who are mentally ill will be noticed and helped far earlier, and those at risk will have many more healthy pathways to health and well-being.

Institutions of higher learning often seem to add to the anxiety in our society by overemphasizing power, external accomplishments, and cognitive pursuits to the detriment of the whole person. We realize it represents a big paradigm shift to put self-knowledge and well-being at the top of an institutions' priorities, but it is the only way to reverse the tragic trends and loss of well-being in our country.

Colleges and universities actually shape society; provide the leaders for our health care, business, and governmental organizations; and lead our system of education. Therefore, higher education's leaders have a moral responsibility to do everything they can to strengthen people's well-being.

Higher education can encourage humanity's deep hunger for expressing contributions to the greater good and the well-being of all. We have evolved as a human species, where now our consciousness is ready to create and witness acts of kindness and love.

Our Journey

We ourselves struggled with purpose and self-knowledge in our college years, although outwardly we were doing fine, and we searched for help from our institutions but did not know enough to ask, or felt stifled talking about human emotions and noncognitive needs in places that appeared to worship academic and intellectual cognition. So we took responsibility in our adult lives to help others who might be in a similar situation.

We believe, and deep inside ourselves know, that we can help by bringing all of the positive developments and knowledge about well-being into the mainstream of the higher education mission. What keeps us motivated is the possibility of actually impacting the human condition, of providing perspectives and approaches that can help people get on track and create pathways to happy, healthy and flourishing lives. We are blessed to have discovered this for ourselves, and we hope to help others with what we have learned.

If you have been helped in some small way, either personally or professionally, by reading this book or using it in your life, you have honored us.

REFERENCES AND ELECTRONIC RESOURCES

Achor, S. 2010. *The Happiness Advantage*. New York: Random House.

American College Personnel Association. 2008. *Professional Competencies: A Report of the Steering Committee on Professional Competencies*. http://www.myacpa.org/au/governance/docs/ACPA_Competencies.pdf

American College Personnel Association & National Association of Student Personnel Administrators. 2010. *ACPA/NASPA Professional Competency Areas for Student Affairs Practitioners*. Washington, DC: Authors. http://www.myacpa.org/professional-competency-areas-student-affairs-practitioners

American Psychiatric Association. 2000. *Diagnostic and Statistical Manual of Mental Disorders* (4th ed.). Arlington, VA: Author.

American Psychiatric Association. 2013. *Diagnostic and Statistical Manual of Mental Disorders* (5th ed.). Washington, DC: Author.

Anderson, J. R., & Lebiere, C. 1998. *The Atomic Components of Thought*. Mahwah, NJ: Lawrence Erlbaum.

Association of American Colleges and Universities. 2002. *Greater Expectations: A New Vision for Learning as the Nation Goes to College*. https://www.aacu.org/sites/default/files/files/publications/GreaterExpectations.pdf

Association of American Universities. 2015. *Report on the AAU Campus Climate Survey on Sexual Assault and Sexual Misconduct*. http://www.aau.edu/Climate-Survey.aspx?id=16525

Baker, D. P. 2014. *The Schooled Society: The Educational Transformation of Global Culture*. Stanford: Stanford University Press.

Bandura, A. 1986. *Social Foundations of Thought and Action: A Social Cognitive Theory*. Englewood Cliffs, NJ: Prentice-Hall.

Bandura, A. 1997. *Self-Efficacy: The Exercise of Control*. New York: Freeman.

Bandura, A., Barbaranelli, C., Caprara, G. V., & Pastorelli, C. 2001. "Self-Efficacy Beliefs as Shapers of Children's Aspirations and Career Trajectories." *Child Development* 72(1): 187–206.

Baumgardner, Ann H. 1990. "To Know Oneself Is to Like Oneself: Self-Certainty and Self-Affect." *Journal of Personality and Social Psychology* 58(6; June 1990): 1062–72.

Berger, K. S., & Thompson, R. A. 1995. *The Developing Person through Childhood and Adolescence.* New York: Worth.

Blume, G. W., & Heckman, D. S. 1997. "What Do Students Know about Algebra and Functions?" In *Results from the Sixth Mathematics Assessment*, edited by P. A. Kenney & E. A. Silver, pp. 225–77. Reston, VA: National Council of Teachers of Mathematics.

Bouffard-Bouchard, T. 1990. Influence of Self-Efficacy on Performance in a Cognitive Task. *Journal of Social Psychology* 130, 353–63.

Brown, F., & LaJambe, C. 2016. *Positive Psychology and Well Being: Applications for Enhanced Living.* San Diego, CA: Cognella.

Brzycki, H. G. 2009. "Teacher Beliefs and Classroom Practices that Impart Self-System and Positive Psychology Attributes." PhD diss., Penn State University. https://etda.libraries.psu.edu/paper/9451/5058

Brzycki, H. G. 2010. "The Self in Teaching and Learning." In *Educational Psychology Reader: The Art and Science of How People Learn*, edited by G. S. Goodman, pp. 681–700. New York: Peter Lang.

Brzycki, H. G. 2013. *The Self in Schooling: Theory and Practice: How to Create Happy, Healthy and Flourishing Children in the 21 Century.* State College, PA: BG Publishing.

Butler County Community College. 2016. *Promoting Student Success and Retention at BC3.* http://www.bc3.edu/services/pdf/oral-presentations.pdf

California State University. 2016. *Academic and Student Success Programs: High Impact Practices Systematically.* Conference at Hotel Fullerton Anaheim. https://www.calstate.edu/engage/conference/documents/2016-ASSP-Conference-program.pdf

Carlstrom, A. (Ed.). 2013. *NACADA National Survey of Academic Advising* (Monograph No. 25). Manhattan, KS: National Academic Advising Association. http://www.nacada.ksu.edu/Resources/Clearinghouse/View-Articles/Advisor-Load.aspx

Center for Collegiate Mental Health. (2016, January). *2015 Annual Report* (Publication No. STA 15-108) http://ccmh.psu.edu/wpcontent/uploads/sites/3058/2016/01/2015_CCMH_Report_1-18-2015.pdf

Center for Community College Student Engagement. 2012. *A Matter of Degrees: Promising Practices for Community College Student Success (A First Look).* Austin, TX: The University of Texas at Austin, Community College Leadership Program.

Centers for Disease Control and Prevention. 2005. "CDC Efforts to Reduce or Prevent Obesity." http://www.cdc.gov/OD/OC/MEDIA/pressrel/fs050419.htm

Centers for Disease Control and Prevention. 2007. "Teen Suicide Rate: Highest Increase in 15 Years." http://www.sciencedaily.com/releases/2007/09/070907221530.htm

Centers for Disease Control and Prevention. 2010. "Current Depression among Adults—United States, 2006 and 2008." *MMWR* 59(38): 1229–35.

Centers for Disease Control and Prevention. 2011. "Antidepressant Use in Persons Aged 12 and Over: United States, 2005–2008." *National Center for Health Statistics Brief*, no 76. http://www.cdc.gov/nchs/data/databriefs/db76.htm

Centers for Disease Control and Prevention. 2011. *Public Health Action Plan to Integrate Mental Health Promotion and Mental Illness Prevention with Chronic Disease Prevention, 2011–2015.* Atlanta: US Department of Health and Human Services.

Centers for Disease Control and Prevention. 2012a. "Adult Obesity Facts." http://www.cdc.gov/obesity/data/adult.html

Centers for Disease Control and Prevention. 2012b. "National Vital Statistics System—Mortality." http://www.cdc.gov/nchs/deaths.htm

Centers for Disease Control and Prevention, Office of Analysis and Epidemiology. 2012. "Identifying Emotional and Behavioral Problems in Children Aged 4–17 Years: United States, 2001–2007," by P. N. Pastor, C. A. Reuben, & C. R. Duran. http://www.ncbi.nlm.nih.gov/pubmed/22737946

Center for Community College Engagement. 2015. "Community College Survey of Student Engagement." The University of Texas at Austin. http://www.ccsse.org/survey/survey.cfm

Cohen, E. 2007. "CDC: Antidepressants Most Prescribed Drug in U.S." http://articles.cnn.com/2007-07-09/health/antidepressants_1_antidepressants-high-blood-pressure-drugs-psychotropic-drugs?_s=PM:HEALTH

Cohen, J. 2006. "Social, Emotional, Ethical, and Academic Education: Creating a Climate for Learning, Participation in Democracy, and Well-Being." *Harvard Educational Review* 76: 2.

Cohen, S., Doyle, W. J., Treanor, J. J., & Turner, R. B. 2006. "Positive Emotional Style Predicts Resistance to Illness after Experimental Exposure to Rhinovirus or Influenza A Virus." *Journal of Bio-Behavioral Medicine* 68(6): 809–15.

Cohen, S., Doyle, W. J., Turner, R. B., Alper, C. M., & Skoner, D. P. 2006. "Research Highlight: Emotional Style and Susceptibility to the Common Cold." In *Healthier Lives through Behavioral and Social Science Research*. Available from the Office of Behavioral and Social Sciences Research website: http://obssr.od.nih.gov/publications/books_and_projects/books_and_reports.aspx.

Collins, J. L. 1982. "Self-Efficacy and Ability in Achievement Behavior." Paper presented at the Annual Meeting of the American Educational Research Association, New York, March.

Cornell University. 2014. "University Launches 'Engaged Cornell' with $50 million Gift." *Cornell Chronicle*. http://news.cornell.edu/stories/2014/10/university-launches-engaged-cornell-50-million-gift

Cornell University. 2015. "Cornell University at Its Sesquicentennial: A Strategic Plan 20102015." https://www.cornell.edu/strategicplan/docs/060410-strategic-plan-summary.pdf

Cornell University. 2016. "Gannett Health Center: Building Resilience." https://www.gannett.cornell.edu/topics/resilience/index.cfm

Couture, R. 2016. *Impactful Advising: Investing in Students' Lives.* Manuscript submitted for publication.
Cremin, L. A. 1964. *The Transformation of the School: Progressivism in American Education 1876–1957.* New York: Vintage/Random House.
Csikszentmihalyi, M. 1993. *The Evolving Self.* New York: HarperCollins.
Csikszentmihalyi, M. 1997. *Creativity: Flow and the Psychology of Discovery and Invention.* New York: HarperCollins.
Curtin, S. C., Warner, M., & Hedegaard, H. 2016. *Increase in Suicide in the United States, 1999–2014.* NCHS data brief no. 241. Hyattsville, MD: National Center for Health Statistics.
Cuseo, J. 2008. "Assessing Advisor Effectiveness." In *Academic Advising: A Comprehensive Handbook* (2nd ed.), edited by V. N. Gordon, W. R. Habley, & T. J. Grites, pp. 369–385. San Francisco: Jossey-Bass.
Damasio, A. 1994. *Descartes' Error: Emotion, Reason, and the Human Brain.* New York: Penguin.
Deci, E. L., & Ryan, R. M. 1985. *Intrinsic Motivation and Self-Determination in Human Behavior.* New York: Cambridge University Press.
Dewey, J. 1900. *The School and Society.* Chicago: University of Chicago Press.
Dewey, J. 1902. *The Child and the Curriculum.* Chicago: University of Chicago Press.
Dewey, J. 1916. *Democracy and Education.* New York: Macmillan.
DiMaggio, P. 1997. "Culture and Cognition." *Annual Review of Sociology* 23: 263–87.
Dowell, D., Haegerich, T. M., & Chou, R. 2016. "CDC Guideline for Prescribing Opioids for Chronic Pain—United States." *MMWR Recomm Rep* 65: 1–49.
Durham, T. 2015. *University of Kansas, Student Affairs Impact Report, 2014–2015.* https://studentaffairs.ku.edu/sites/studentaffairs.ku.edu/files/docs/SA_Impact_Report%20Final_2015.pdf
Eagan, K., Stolzenberg, E. B., Ramirez, J. J., Aragon, M. C., Suchard, M. R., & Hurtado, S. 2014. *The American Freshman: National Norms, Fall 2014.* Los Angeles: Higher Education Research Institute, UCLA. http://www.heri.ucla.edu
Edwards, V. J., Anda, R. F., Dube, S. R., Dong, M., Chapman, D. F., & Felitti, V. J. 2005. "The Wide-Ranging Health Consequences of Adverse Childhood Experiences." In *Victimization of Children and Youth: Patterns of Abuse, Response Strategies*, edited by K. Kendall-Tackett & S. Giacomoni. Kingston, NJ: Civic Research Institute.
Erikson, E. 1963. *Childhood and Society.* New York: Norton.
Erikson, E. 1968. *Identity, Youth, and Crisis.* New York: Norton.
Erikson, E. 1980. *Identity and the Life Cycle.* New York: Norton.
Falce, L. May 2016. "Penn State Sees Increase in Self-Injury Cases, Suicidal Ideation." *Centre Daily Times.* http://www.centredaily.com/news/local/education/penn-state/article75776342.html#storylink=cpy
Farrington, C. A. April 2013. *Academic Mindsets as a Critical Component of Deeper Learning.* White paper prepared for the William and Flora Hewlett Foundation.

Felitti, V. J., & Anda, R. F., 2009. "The Relationship of Adverse Childhood Experiences to Adult Medical Disease, Psychiatric Disorders, and Sexual Behavior: Implications for Healthcare." In *The Hidden Epidemic: The Impact of Early Life Trauma on Health and Disease*, edited by R. Lanius & E. Vermetten. Cambridge: Cambridge University Press. http://www.unnaturalcauses.org/assets/uploads/file/ACE%20Study-Lanius.pdf

Felitti, V. J., Anda, R. F., Nordenberg, D., Williamson, D. F., Spitz, A. M., Edwards, V., Koss, M. P., & Marks, J. S. 1998. "Relationship of Childhood Abuse and Household Dysfunction to Many of the Leading Causes of Death in Adults: The Adverse Childhood Experiences (ACE) Study." *American Journal of Preventive Medicine* 14: 245–58.

Festinger, L. 1957. *A Theory of Cognitive Dissonance*. Stanford: Stanford University Press.

Florida State University. 2016. *The Center for Academic Retention and Enhancement* (CARE). http://care.fsu.edu/College-Programs/CARE-College-Life-Coaching

Gardner, H. 1983. *Frames of Mind: The Theory of Multiple Intelligences*. New York: Basic Books.

Glennen, R. E. 1975. "Intrusive College Counseling." *College Student Journal* 9(1). http://www.nacada.ksu.edu/Resources/Academic-Advising-Today/View-Articles/Proactive-(Intrusive)-Advising!.aspx#sthash.ZLRKeRko.dpuf

Goetz, T., Zirngibl, A., Pekrun, R., & Hall, N. 2003. "Emotions, Learning and Achievement from an Educational-Psychological Perspective." In *Learning Emotions: The Influence of Affective Factors on Classroom Learning*, edited by P. Mayring & C. von Rhoeneck, pp. 9–28. Frankfurt, Germany: Peter Lang.

Goleman, D. 1995. *Emotional Intelligence: Why It Can Matter More than IQ*. New York: Bantam Books.

Grites, T. J. 2013. "Developmental Academic Advising: A 40-Year Context." *NACADA Journal* 33(1): 5–15. http://www.nacada.ksu.edu/Resources/Journal/Download-Journal-Articles.aspx

Harter, S. 1999. *The Construction of the Self: A Developmental Perspective*. New York: Guilford Press.

Harter, S., & Marold, D. 1992. "Psychosocial Risk Factors Contributing to Adolescent Suicidal Ideation." In *Child and Adolescent Suicide: Clinical Developmental Perspectives*, edited by G. Noam & S. Borst. Rochester, NY: University of Rochester Press.

Hawkins, D. J., Kosterman, R., Catalano, R. F., Hill, K. G., & Abbott, R. D. 2008. "Effects of Social Development Intervention in Childhood 15 Years Later." *Archives of Pediatric and Adolescent Medicine* 162(12): 1133–41.

Henriques, G. 2014. "The College Student Mental Health Crisis." *Psychology Today*. https://www.psychologytoday.com/blog/theory-knowledge/201402/the-college-student-mental-health-crisis

Hiebert, J., & Carpenter, T. 1992. "Learning and Teaching with Understanding." In *Handbook of Research on Mathematics Teaching and Learning*, edited by D. Grouws, pp. 65–97. New York: Simon & Schuster Macmillan.

Hillman, J. 1996. *The Soul's Code: In Search of Character and Calling*. New York: Random House.

Hillman, J. 1999. *The Force of Character and the Lasting Life*. New York: Random House.

Hoffman, J. L., & Bresciani, M. J. (2012). "Identifying What Student Affairs Professionals Value: A Mixed Methods Analysis of Professional Competencies Listed in Job Descriptions." *Research and Practice in Assessment*, 7(1), 26–40. http://go.galegroup.com/ps/i.do?id=GALE%7CA339254319&v=2.1&u=ksu&it=r&p=AONE&sw=w&asid=3a8f2f636f2ee220a73aacafa511ac74

Immordino-Yang, M. H., & Damasio, A. 2007. "We Feel, Therefore We Learn: The Relevance of Affective and Social Neuroscience to Education." *Mind, Brain, and Education* 1(1): 3–10.

Indiana University Center for Postsecondary Research. 2015. *The Carnegie Classification of Institutions of Higher Education, 2015 edition*, Bloomington, IN: Author.

International Assessments of Counseling Services (IACS). 2014. *Standards for University and College Counseling Services*. Alexandria, VA: Author. http://0201.nccdn.net/1_2/000/000/0ce/fa4/IACS-STANDARDS-updated-9-24-2015.pdf

International Association of Counseling Services. 2014. *National Survey of College Counseling Centers*. Monograph Series Number 9V. http://www.collegecounseling.org/wp-content/uploads/NCCCS2014_v2.pdf

Jahoda, M. 1958. *Current Concepts of Positive Mental Health*. New York: Basic Books.

James, W. 1890. *Principles of Psychology* (vol. 1). New York: Henry Holt and Company.

James, W. 1892. *Psychology (Briefer Course)*. New York: The Library of America.

Jung, C. G. 1961. *Memories, Dreams, Reflections*, edited by Aniela Jaffé. New York: Vintage Books.

Kegan, J. 1994. *In Over Our Heads: The Mental Demands of Modern Life*. Cambridge, MA: Harvard University Press.

Keltner, D. 2009. *Born to Be Good*. New York: Norton.

Kroger, J. 1996. "Identity, Regression and Development." *Journal of Adolescence* 19: 203–22.

Kuh, G. D. 2008. *High-Impact Educational Practices: What They Are, Who Has Access to Them, and Why They Matter*. AAC&U. http://www.aacu.org/leap/hips

Kuhn, T. L. (2008). "Historical Foundations of Academic Advising." In *Academic Advising: A Comprehensive Handbook* (2nd ed.), edited by V. N. Gordon, W. R. Habley, & T. J. Grites. San Francisco: Jossey-Bass.

Kyllonen, P. C. 2005. *The Case for Non-cognitive Assessments*. Princeton, NJ: ETS Research & Development, Educational Testing Service. https://www.ets.org/Media/Research/pdf/RD_Connections3.pdf

Lent, R. W., Brown, S. D., & Larkin, K. C. 1984. "Relation of Self-Efficacy Expectations to Academic Achievement and Persistence." *Journal of Counseling Psychology*, 31, 356–62.

Lent, R. W., Singley, D., Sheu, H., & Gainor, K. 2005. "Social Cognitive Predictors of Domain and Life Satisfaction: Exploring the Theoretical Precursors of Subjective Well-Being." *Journal of Counseling Psychology* 52(3): 429–42.

Locke, B. "Need for Mental Health Awareness, Funding for College Students Grows." *Centre Daily Times*, May 21, 2016. http://www.centredaily.com/living/article79022677.html

Locker, J., & Cropley, M. 2004. "Anxiety, Depression and Self-Esteem in Secondary School Children: An Investigation into the Impact of Standard Assessment Tests (SATs) and Other Important School Examinations." *School Psychology International* 25(3): 333–45.

Lopez, S. 2009. *Hope, Academic Success, and the Gallup Student Poll*. Omaha, NE: Gallup.

Lumina Foundation. 2015. *Who Is Today's Student?* https://www.luminafoundation.org/todays-student-statistics

Magolda, M.B. (2010). "The Interweaving of Epistemological, Intrapersonal, and Interpersonal Development in the Evolution of Self-Authorship." In *Development and Assessment of Self-Authorship*, edited by M. B. Magolda, E. F. Creamer, & P. S. Meszaros, pp. 25–43. Sterling, VA: Stylus Publishing.

Mann, M., Hosman, C. M. H., Schaalma, H. P., & de Vries, N. K. 2004. "Self-Esteem in a Broad Spectrum Approach for Mental Health Promotion." *Health Education Research: Theory and Practice* 19(4): 357–72.

Marcia, J. E. 1966. "Development and Validation of the Ego Identity Status." *Journal of Personality and Social Psychology* 3: 551–58.

Marcia, J. E. 1991. "Identity and Self Development." In *Encyclopedia of Adolescence* (vol. 1), edited by R. Lerner, A. Peterson, & J. Brooks-Gunn. New York: Garland.

Marcia, J. E. 2002. "Identity and Psychosocial Development in Adulthood." *Identity: An International Journal of Theory and Research* 2:7–28.142.

Marcia, J. E., Waterman, A. S., Matteson, D. R., Archer, S. L., & Orlofsky, J. L. 1993. *Ego Identity*. New York: Springer.

Marks, L. J., & Wade, J. C. 2015. "Positive Psychology on Campus: Creating the Conditions for Well-Being and Success," *About Campus*, January/February, pp. 9–15.

Markus, H. 1977. "Self-Schemata and Processing Information about the Self." *Journal of Personality and Social Psychology* 35: 63–78.

Markus, H., & Nurius, P. 1986. "Possible Selves." *American Psychologist* 41(9): 954–69.

Maslow, A. H. 1943. "A Theory of Human Motivation." *Psychological Review*, 50, 370–96.

Maslow, A. H. 1954. *Motivation and Personality*. New York: Harper and Row.

Maslow, A. H. 1968. *Toward a Psychology of Being*. New York: John Wiley & Sons.

McDevitt, T. M., & Ormrod, J. E. 2007. *Child Development and Education*, 3rd ed. Upper Saddle River, NJ: Pearson Education.

Mink, O., Owen, K., & Mink, B. 1993. *Developing High-Performance People: The Art of Coaching*. Reading, MA: Addison-Wesley.

Moscovitch, M., & Craik, F. I. M. 1976. "Depth of Processing, Retrieval Cues, and Uniqueness of Encoding as a Factor in Recall." *Journal of Verbal Learning and Verbal Behavior* 15: 447–58.

National Alliance on Mental Health. (2012). *College Students Speak: A Survey Report on Mental Health.* Written by D. Gruttadaro and D. Crudo. http://www.nami.org/namioncampus/

National Association of Colleges and Employers. 2013. *The Professional Standards for College and University Career Services.* http://www.naceweb.org/knowledge/career-services-competencies.aspx

National Career Development Association (NACADA). 2005. *NACADA Statement of Core Values of Academic Advising.* http://www.nacada.ksu.edu/Resources/Clearinghouse/View-Articles/Core-values-of-academic-advising.aspx

National Career Development Association (NACADA). 2009. *National Career Development Guidelines (NCDG) Framework.* http://www.ncda.org/aws/NCDA/asset_manager/get_file/3384/ncdguidelines2007.pdf

National Institute of Mental Health. 2010. "National Survey Confirms That Youth Are Disproportionately Affected by Mental Disorders." http://www.nimh.nih.gov/science-news/2010/national-survey-confirms-that-youth-are-disproportionately-affected-by-mental-disorders.shtml

National Institute of Mental Health. 2011. "Borderline Personality Disorder Definition and Statistics." http://www.nimh.nih.gov/statistics/1Borderline.shtml

National Survey of Student Engagement. 2007. *Experiences That Matter: Enhancing Student Learning and Success—Annual Results 2007.* Bloomington, IN: Indiana University Center for Postsecondary Research. http://nsse.indiana.edu/NSSE_2007_Annual_Report/docs/withhold/NSSE_2007_Annual_Report.pdf

National Survey of Student Engagement. 2013. *A Fresh Look at Student Engagement—Annual Results 2013.* Bloomington, IN: Indiana University Center for Postsecondary Research. http://nsse.indiana.edu/nsse_2013_results/pdf/nsse_2013_annual_results.pdf

National Survey of Student Engagement. 2015. *Engagement Insights: Survey Findings on the Quality of Undergraduate Education—Annual Results 2015.* Bloomington, IN: Indiana University Center for Postsecondary Research. http://nsse.indiana.edu/NSSE_2015_Results/pdf/NSSE_2015_Annual_Results.pdf

Neuman, S. B., Copple, C., & Bredekamp, S. 1998. "Learning to Read and Write: Developmentally Appropriate Practices for Young Children. A Joint Position Statement of the International Reading Association (IRA) and the National Association for the Education of Young Children (NAEYC)." http://oldweb.naeyc.org/about/positions/pdf/PSREAD98.PDF

Odum, H. T. 1988. "Self-Organization, Transformity, and Information." *Science* 242: 1132–1139.

Ohio State University. 2015. *Office of Student Life Wellness Assessment.* http://cssl.osu.edu/posts/documents/wellness-assessment-report-january-2015.pdf

Orth, U., Robbins, R. W., & Widaman, K. F. 2012. "Life-Span Development of Self-Esteem and Its Effects on Important Life Outcomes." *Journal of Personality and Social Psychology* 102(6): 1271–88.
Oyserman, D., & James, L. 2009. "Possible Selves: From Content to Process." In *The Handbook of Imagination and Mental Stimulation*, edited by K. D. Markman, W. M. Klein, & J. A. Suhr. New York: Psychology Press.
Parjares, M. F. 1992. "Teachers Beliefs and Educational Research: Cleaning Up a Messy Construct." *Review of Educational Research* 62: 307–32.
Parjares, M. F. 1996. "Self-Efficacy Beliefs in Academic Settings." *Review of Educational Research* 66(4): 543–78.
The Pennsylvania State University. 2014. *PSU High Impact Practice: Greening of Philadelphia* Service Learning. http://h2oblues.org/themes/penn-state/penn-state-philadelphia-event
The Pennsylvania State University. (January 2015). *The Pennsylvania State University Task Force on Sexual Assault and Sexual Harassment Report*. http://www.psu.edu/ur/2014/Task_Force_final_report.pdf
The Pennsylvania State University. (April 2016a). *The Sexual Misconduct Climate Survey*. https://studentaffairs.psu.edu/assessment/SMCS/
The Pennsylvania State University. (April 2016b). *WPSU Higher Education: Evaluating Mental Health on Campus*. Television broadcast. http://wpsu.psu.edu/tv/programs/infocus/evaluating-mental-health-on-campus
The Pennsylvania State University. 2016. *The Pennsylvania State University's Strategic Plan for 2016 to 2020*. http://www.psu.edu/trustees/pdf/Penn%20State%20Strategic%20Plan%202016-2020%20-%20CoGLRP%20Review%2001-04-16.pdf
Piaget, J. 1968. *Six Psychological Studies*. New York: Random House.
Pintrich, P. R., & Schunk, D. H. 2002. *Motivation in Education: Theory, Research, and Applications*. Upper Saddle River, NJ: Prentice-Hall.
Reeder, G. D., McCormick, C. B., & Esselman, E. D. 1987. "Self-Referent Processing and Recall of Prose." *Journal of Educational Psychology* 79(3): 243–48.
Robinson, K. 2001. *Out of Our Minds: Learning to Be Creative*. West Sussex: Capstone.
Rogers, C. 1954. "Toward a Theory of Creativity." *ETC: A Review of General Semantics* 11: 249–60.
Rogers, C. 1961. *On Becoming a Person*. Boston: Houghton Mifflin.
Rogers, C. 1980. *A Way of Being*. Boston: Houghton Mifflin.
Rogers, C. 1986. "A Client-Centered/Person-Centered Approach to Therapy." In *The Carl Rogers Reader*, edited by H. Kirschenbaum & V. Land Henderson. Boston: Houghton Mifflin.
Rogers, P. 2011. *Understanding Risk and Protective Factors for Suicide: A Primer for Preventing Suicide*. Washington, DC: Substance Abuse and Mental Health Services Administration (SAMSHA) Suicide Prevention Resource Center (SPRC). http://www.sprc.org/sites/sprc.org/files/library/RiskProtectiveFactorsPrimer.pdf

Rogers, T. B., Kuiper, N. A., & Kirker, W. S. 1977. "Self-Reference and the Encoding of Personal Information." *Journal of Personality and Social Psychology* 35: 677–88.

Rotter, J. B. 1966. "Generalized Expectancies for Internal Versus External Control of Reinforcement." *Psychological Monographs* 80(1): 1–28.

Ryan, R. M., & Deci, E. 2000. "Self-Determination Theory and the Facilitation of Intrinsic Motivation, Social Development, and Well-Being." *American Psychologist* 55: 68–78.

Ryan, R. M., & Deci, E. L. 2001. "On Happiness and Human Potentials: A Review of Research on Hedonic and Eudaimonic Well-Being." *Annual Review of Psychology* 52: 141–66.

Ryff, C. D., & Singer, B. 1998a. "The Contours of Positive Human Health." *Psychological Inquiry* 9: 1–28.

Ryff, C. D., & Singer, B. 1998b. "The Role of Purpose in Life and Personal Growth in Positive Human Health." In *The Human Quest for Meaning: A Handbook of Psychological Research and Clinical Applications*, edited by P. T. P. Wong & P. S. Fry, pp. 213–35. Mahwah, NJ: Lawrence Erlbaum.

Ryff, C. D., & Singer, B. 2003. "The Role of Emotion on Pathways to Positive Health." In *Handbook of Affective Sciences*, edited by R. J. Davidson, K. R. Scherer, & H. H. Goldsmith. New York: Oxford University Press.

Ryff, C. D., Singer, B., Love, G. D., & Essex, M. J. 1998. "Resilience in Adulthood and Later Life: Defining Features and Dynamic Processes." In *Handbook of Aging and Mental Health*, edited by J. Lomranz. New York: Plenum.

Scheffler, I. 1985. *Of Human Potential*. Boston: Routledge & Kegan Paul.

Schreiner L., & Anderson, E. 2005. Strengths based advising: A new lens for higher education. *NACADA Journal*, 25(2), 20–29.

Seifert, T.A. 2005. *The Ryff Scales of Psychological Well-Being*. Center for Inquiry at Wabash University. http://www.liberalarts.wabash.edu/ryff-scales/

Seligman, M. E. P. 2011. *Flourish: A Visionary New Understanding of Happiness and Well-Being*. New York: Free Press.

Seligman, M. E. P., & Csikszentmihalyi, M. 2000. "Positive Psychology: An Introduction." *American Psychologist* 55: 5–14.

Seligman, M. E. P., Schulman, P., DeRubeis, R. J., & Hollon, S. D. (1999). "The Prevention of Depression and Anxiety." *Prevention & Treatment*, 2(1), December: 8a. http://dx.doi.org/10.1037/1522-3736.2.1.28a

Selingo, J. 2015. *Student Success: Building a Culture for Retention and Completion on College Campuses*. Washington, DC: The Chronicle of Higher Education.

Shankman, M. L., Allen, S. J., and Miguel, R. 2015.*Emotionally Intelligent Leadership for Students: Inventory*, 2nd ed. San-Francisco: Jossey-Bass

Shouse, E. 2005. "Feeling, Emotion, Affect." http://journal.media culture.org.au/0512/03-shouse.php

Silvergate, H. (2016). "Harvard to Supply Life's Meaning to Students." *Minding the Campus*, March. http://www.mindingthecampus.org/2016/03/harvard-to-supply-lifes-meaning-to-students/

Snyder, C. R., & Lopez, S. J., eds. 2005. *Handbook of Positive Psychology.* London: Oxford University Press.
Snyder, C. R., Rand, K. L., & Sigmon, D. R. 2005. "Hope Theory: A Member of the Positive Psychology Family." In *Handbook of Positive Psychology*, edited by C. R. Snyder & S. J. Lopez, pp. 257–76. London: Oxford University Press.
Stanford University. 2016. *Designing Your Life.* http://www.stanford.edu/class/me104b/cgi-bin/
Sternberg, R. J. 2013. "Research to Improve Retention Inside Higher Ed." https://www.insidehighered.com/views/2013/02/07/essay-use-research-improve-student-retention#ixzz2QAelwRP5
St. Petersburg College. 2015. *The College Experience.* http://www.spcollege.edu/collegeexperience/
St. Petersburg College. 2016. *My Learning Plan.* Student success white paper. http://www.spcollege.edu/SACS_COC/artifacts/2.10_Student_Support_Services/MyLearningPlanWhitepaper.pdf
Suicide Prevention Resource Center. 2014. *Suicide among College and University Students in the United States.* Waltham, MA: Education Development Center.
Swarbrick, M. 2006. "A Wellness Approach." *Psychiatric Rehabilitation Journal* 29(4): 311–14.
Taylor Huber, M., & Hutchings, P. 2004. *Integrative Learning: Mapping the Terrain.* Washington, DC: Association of American Colleges and Universities and the Carnegie Foundation for the Advancement of Teaching. http://archive.carnegiefoundation.org/pdfs/elibrary/elibrary_pdf_636.pdf
Ternouth, A., Collier, D., & Maughan, B. 2009. "Childhood Emotional Problems and Self-Perceptions Predict Weight Gain in a Longitudinal Regression Model." *BMC Medicine* 7: 46.
Tinto, V. 2004. "Linking Learning and Leaving." In *Reworking the Student Departure Puzzle*, edited by J. M. Braxton. Nashville, TN: Vanderbilt University Press.
Twenge, J. M., & Campbell, K. W. 2009. T*he Narcissism Epidemic: Living in the Age of Entitlement.* New York: Free Press.
Twenge, J. M., Gentile, B., DeWall, C. N., Ma, D. S., Lacefield, K., & Schurtz, D. R. 2010. "Birth Cohort Increases in Psychopathology among Young Americans, 1938–2007: A Cross-Temporal Meta-Analysis of the MMPI." *Clinical Psychology Review* 30: 145–54.
University of Central Florida. 2016. "Counseling and Psychological Services: Therapist Assisted Online (TAO)." http://caps.sdes.ucf.edu/tao
University of Kansas Student Affairs. *Student Affairs Impact Report.* http://studentaffairs.ku.edu/sites/studentaffairs.ku.edu/files/docs/SA_Impact_Report%20Final_2015.pdf
University of Michigan. 2016a. "Newnan Academic Advising Center Student Success Workshops." http://www.lsa.umich.edu/advising/academicsupport/strategiesforsuccess/healthandwellness

University of Michigan. 2016b. "Integrative Learning in Student Life." https://studentlife.umich.edu/research/article/integrative-learning-student-life-part-iii

University of Michigan. 2016c. "Integrative Learning in Student Life: Student Life Research Video." https://studentlife.umich.edu/integrative-learning

University of Pennsylvania. 2015. "Report of the Task Force on Student Psychological Health and Welfare." *UPenn Almanac*. http://www.upenn.edu/almanac/volumes/v61/n23/pdf/task-force-psychological-health.pdf

US Congress. 2013. "Violence Against Women Reauthorization Act (VAWA)." Washington, DC: United States Publishing Office. https://www.gpo.gov/fdsys/pkg/BILLS-113s47enr/pdf/BILLS-113s47enr.pdf

US Department of Education, National Center for Education Statistics. 2015. *The Condition of Education 2015 (NCES 2015-144): Institutional Retention and Graduation Rates for Undergraduate Students*. Washington, DC: Author.

US Department of Education, National Center for Education Statistics. 2009. *Beginning Postsecondary Survey*. Washington, DC: Author.

Varney, J. (2012). "Proactive (Intrusive) Advising!" *Academic Advising Today*, 35(3; September). http://www.nacada.ksu.edu/Resources/Academic-Advising-Today/View-Articles/Proactive-(Intrusive)-Advising!.aspx#

Wade, J. C., Marks, L. I., & Hetzel, R. D. (eds.). 2015. *Positive Psychology on the College Campus*. New York: Oxford University Press.

Wallis, C. 2005. "The New Science of Happiness." *Time*, January 17. http://content.time.com/time/magazine/article/0,9171,1015832,00.html

Wilkins, J. 2015. *Students' Perceptions of their First-Year Experience in Relation to Support They Receive from an Urban Mid-sized Public College*. Internal study and presentation. joshuawilkin@gmail.com

Willoughby, C. 2015. "Theoretical Design and Real World Outcomes for New Student Orientation." Presented at the Theory to Practice to Outcomes: Connecting Student Development Theory to Community College Practice Conference, Morgan State University, Maryland.

Willoughby, C. 2016a. *Student Success at Butler County Community College*. Internal white paper.

Willoughby, C. 2016b. *BC3 Welcome Day 2013–2014 Report*. Internal white paper.

Winston, R. B., Jr., Miller, T. K., Ender, S. C., Grites, T. J., & associates (eds.). 1984. *Developmental Academic Advising*. San Francisco: Jossey-Bass.

Yancy, K. B. 2004. *Teaching Literature as Reflective Practice*. Urbana, IL: National Council of Teachers of English.

INDEX

abusive behavior, 21
academic advising, xi, 30, 31, 35, 37, 41,
    52, 55, 79, 81, 96, 97, 98, 101, 109,
    119, 131, 138, 143, 144, 153
    professional standards, 55
    and student individual beliefs,
        potential, self-reliance, and
        self-management, 55
    promising practices
        individualized student learning
            plans (Center for the Self in
            Schools), 134–35
        online assessments (ePortfolios),
            135–36
        workshop series on student success
            dimensions (University of
            Michigan), 133
    student success professional standards
        National Academic Advising
            Association (NACADA),
            64–66, 75, 131
academic affairs, 18
academic learning, 35
academic mind-set, 103
achievement, 25
    and goals, 34
Achor, Shawn, 1
adverse childhood experiences (ACE), 20, 27
aggressive behavior, 5
alcohol abuse, 4, 21, 45, 81
American College Health Association
    (2015 survey), 9

American College Personnel Association
    (ACPA), viii
    student success professional
        standards, 58–63, 75, 151
    whole person, 1
American Freshman Survey, The, (2014), 2
American Public University, 117
anxiety, students', 2, 3, 5, 6, 7, 8, 9, 23, 27,
    37, 47, 60, 80, 89, 93, 99, 133, 143,
    144, 146, 159
appreciative inquiry (AI), 98–101
Arkansas Technical University, 96
Association of American Colleges and
    Universities (AAC&U), viii, 56
    and integrative learning, 38–39
    student success professional
        standards, 73–75
        essential learning outcomes, 73–75
        Figure 2—AAC&U Essential
            Learning Outcomes
            Diagram, 73
Association of American Universities
    Campus Survey (AAU) (2015), 10

Baker, David, 1,
Bandura, Albert, 27, 87
beliefs
    personal, 26
    students', 3
borderline personality disorder (BPD),
    99, 100

Brown, Frederick, 23, 82, 162
and *iSelf*, 82
Brown University, 153
Bryant University, 42
Brzycki Group, The
summer bridge program using the *iSelf* model (career counseling high-impact practice), 138–39
Butler County Community College, 120–22
fostering self-direction through first-year seminars (faculty teaching promising practice), 120–22

California State University System, 39
and Latino students, 39
career advising/counseling, xi, 35, 55, 81
high-impact practices
aligning life purpose and career using the *Success Predictor* (Center for the Self in Schools), 138
integrating career counseling and internships using the *iSuccess* model (The Pennsylvania State University), 140–41
summer bridge program using the *iSelf* model (The Brzycki Group), 138–39
professional standards, 55
and positive self-concept, self-assessment, and self-regulation, 55–56
promising practices
Designing Your Life Course (Stanford University), 137
integrating career and academic advising (St. Petersburg), 136–37
student success professional standards
National Association of Colleges and Employers (NACE), 72
National Career Development Association (NCDA), 70–72
career services. *See* career advising/counseling
Carnegie Foundation for Teaching, viii, 39, 119, 133
Center for Collegiate Mental Health (2016), 7
Center for the Self in Schools, The
aligning life purpose and career using the *Success Predictor* (career counseling high-impact practice), 138
individualized student learning plans (faculty teaching promising practice), 134–35
well-being workshops using the *iSelf* model (counseling and psychological services high-impact practice), 145–46
Centers for Disease Control and Prevention, United States (CDC), 8, 21
changing lifestyles to reduce opiates use, 47
mind-body research, 21
Chronicle of Higher Education, 18
and student success (2015), 18
and student success activities, 36
Clarion University of Pennsylvania, 17, 129, 141, 146
teaching with *Self Across the Curriculum* (faculty teaching high-impact practice), 127–28
coaching (life, student success, holistic), 36, 66, 70, 97, 98, 114, 127, 132, 134, 137, 142, 143, 153
cognition
and emotions, 82, 116
cognitive
factors, 40, 52, 1305 (*see also* noncognitive factors)
functioning, 34

cognitive dissonance, 4
college and career readiness, 3, 17
college learning careers, 30, 35
community college, xiii
Community College Survey of Student Engagement (CCSSE), viii, 105
completion rates. *See* retention
consciousness, xii, xiii, 4, 9, 15, 79, 80, 88, 92, 93, 106, 110, 111, 112, 124, 126, 158, 159
Cornell University, 40, 41, 146, 147
 the engaged university (student engagement promising practice), 146–47
 Gannett Health Services Center, 40
 promoting resilience, 40, 41
 teaching both cognitive and noncognitive factors, 40
 mission to teach life skills, 40
Council for the Advancement of Standards (CAS), viii, 66
 student success professional standards, 66–68
counseling and psychological services (CAPS), xi, 35, 55, 81
 high-impact practice
 well-being workshops using the *iSelf* model (Center for the Self in Schools), 145–46
 personal counseling
 promising practices
 focus on life purpose (Harvard University), 142
 life coaching and student success coaching (Florida State University), 142–43
 online therapy (University of Florida), 143–44
 student wellness across the university (The Ohio State University), 144

student success professional standards
 Council for the Advancement of Standards (CAS), 66–68
 International Association of Counseling Services (IACS), 68–70
Couture, Rene, 96
creativity, 95
Csikszentmihalyi, Mihaly, 90, 95
curricular and co-curricular programming, 81
curriculum, 29
 delivered, 29
 experience, 29
 and integrative learning, 39
 lived, 29
 Self Across the Curriculum (SAC)
cutting, 5, 81

Deci, Edward, 90, 94
Department of Education
 National Center for Education Statistics (2009), 17
 National Center for Education Statistics (2015), 18
depression, 3, 4, 6, 7, 8, 9, 12, 21, 27, 47, 60, 61, 80, 81, 87, 89, 94, 99, 159
 adolescent, 8
 children, 8
despair, students', 2, 7
developmental advising, 37–38, 96, 97
Dewey, John, 84, 86
Diagnostic Statistical Manual IV (DSM-IV), 99, 100
Diagnostic Statistical Manual V (DSM-V), 5, 28
dissociation, 5, 9
dreams, xii, xiv, 4, 5, 8, 19, 52, 60, 64, 65, 78, 80, 82, 83, 85, 90, 91, 93, 98, 99, 100, 102, 107, 108, 109, 111, 116, 120, 123, 127, 130, 134, 138, 139, 143, 148, 150

dreams (*continued*)
  envisioning a better world and life, 21
  importance of, 21
dropout rates. *See* retention
drugs, 5
  abuse, 5, 21, 45, 81
  opiates, 8
    CDC lifestyle recommendations, 47
  prescription, 8

emotional intelligence, 20, 41, 75, 83, 85, 91, 94, 95, 108
  and Dr. Henry G. Brzycki, 130, 149, 145
  and Dr. Matthew Shupp, 124, 125, 126, 127
emotions, xi, 9, 10, 12, 14, 24, 26, 29, 33, 34, 41, 60, 81, 82, 83, 89, 90, 91, 93, 94, 96, 98, 111, 114, 115, 116, 126, 127, 152, 160
  and cognition, 82, 116
  positive, 33, 94
Emporia State University, 33
Erikson, Erik, 88

Faculty Survey of Student Engagement (FSSE), viii, 101, 104, 105
  iSelf and *SAC* adding value to, 105–6
faculty teaching, xi, 35, 55, 81
  high-impact practices
    enhancing human development courses with the *iSelf* model (high-impact practice, Clarion University), 129–31
    Figure 6—Three Stages of Development Diagram, 130
    teaching with *Self Across the Curriculum* (high-impact practice, Clarion University), 127–28

professional development for mental health and well-being, 106
professional standards
  and student discernment of ethics, 56
  and student self-understanding, 56
promising practices
  fostering self-direction through first-year seminars (Butler County Community College), 120–21
  student success course (Shippensburg University), 123–27
  student success professional standards
    Association of American Colleges and Universities (AAC&U), 73–75
    essential learning outcomes, 73–75
    Figure 2—AAC&U Essential Learning Outcomes Diagram, 73
first-year programs, 42
  Bryant University, 42
    Wilkin, Joshua, 42
  Butler County Community College, 121–22
  and positive psychology, 42
five student success functions, xi, 35, 55, 81
  self-development educational programming, 46
  See also academic advising; career advising/counseling; counseling and psychological services (CAPS); faculty teaching; student engagement
Florida State University, 142, 143, 147
  life coaching and student success coaching (counseling and psychological services promising practice), 142–43

Gallup and Purdue University poll (2014), 34
Gardner, Howard, 86
  Theory of Multiple Intelligences, 86
Generation Z (GenZ), 15, 92
goodness, human, xi
graduation rates. *See* retention
greater good, xi, xii, 34, 74, 75, 79, 84, 91, 95, 101, 159
Grites, Thomas, 37, 97
  and developmental advising, 37–38, 97
  and holistic view, 38

happiness, 22, 25, 92–93
  and whole person, 31
Harter, Susan, 85–86
Harvard University, 1, 10, 15, 90, 142
  focus on life purpose (counseling and psychological services promising practice), 142
High Point University, 143
higher education
  and the decline of well-being, 1–22
  new mission, 33–53
  responsibilities to serve students and society, 33
high-impact practices, xi, xiii, xiv, xv, 3, 16, 20, 21, 36, 39, 44, 48, 51, 53, 66, 70, 75, 77–17, 119, 120, 123, 127, 129, 138, 140, 142, 145, 148, 149, 152, 155, 158
  to address well-being, 21
  applicable to all Carnegie-classified IHEs, 119
  career counseling
    aligning life purpose and career using the *Success Predictor* (Center for the Self in Schools*)*, 138
    integrating career counseling and internships using the *iSuccess* model (The Pennsylvania State University), 140–41
    summer bridge program using the *iSelf* model (The Brzycki Group), 138–39
  counseling and psychological services (CAPS)
    well-being workshops using the *iSelf* model (Center for the Self in Schools), 145–46
  faculty teaching
    enhancing human development courses with the *iSelf* model (Clarion University), 129–31
    teaching with *Self Across the Curriculum* (Clarion University), 127–28
  iSuccess high-impact practices as compared to Kuh's educational practices, 56, 57, 77
  iSuccess high-impact practices as compared to promising practices, 116
  student engagement
    integrating student engagement through university themes (The Pennsylvania State University), 148–50
Hillman, James, 31
holistic, xv, 29, 38
  approaches to student success, 29
  needs of students, 16, 37
  and student wellness, 21
human development, 9. *See also* individual development
humanistic psychology, 34, 95

identity, 39, 60, 61, 62, 67, 85, 86, 88, 89, 100, 124, 130, 140, 148, 152, 159

individual development, 30, 34
  as part of student success, 30
  self-knowledge as part of, 30
  well-being as part of, 30
inner thoughts and feelings, 9
  and sense of hope, 33–34
inspiration, hopes, and dreams, xii, 93
institutions of higher education (IHEs), xii, 46, 48
  gap between prevention and treatment, 44–46
  gap between student success mission and practice, 49–50
  need for new approaches, 48
Integrated Self model (*iSelf*), xiv, 78, 83–101
  as framework for educators, 84
  as lens, 80
  component parts, 85
  Figure 4—The *iSelf* model, 85
  positive psychology attributes, 84, 90–96
    creativity, 95
    emotional intelligence and positive emotions, 94
    happiness, 92
    inspiration, hope, and dreams, 93
    intrinsic motivation, 92
    life purpose and spirituality, 91
    life meaning, 92
    possible selves, 94
    self-determination, 94
    well-being, 95
  self-system attributes, 84, 85–90
    identity, 88
    locus of control, 89
    self-affect, 90
    self-concept, 86
    self-efficacy, 87
    self-esteem, 86
    self-schema, 89
    self-understanding, 87
  implementation, 96

coaching, 97
developmental and intrusive advising, 96
strengths-based counseling and appreciative inquiry, 98
Integrated Student Success model (*iSuccess*), xiv, 31, 78
  Figure 3—*Integrated Student Success* model (*iSuccess*), 78
  and holistic needs of students, 37
  integrating the five student success functions, 31
  integrating student self-knowledge, 31
  and new ways of thinking, 51
  self-development educational programming, 46
  as student success framework for IHEs, 48
integrative learning, 38–40
  Taylor, Huber, and Hutchings (2004), 39
intellectual growth
  as part of student success, 30
internal versus external selves, 19–21
  self as mediator between, 116
International Association of Counseling Services (IACS), viii, 75
  student success professional standards, 68–70
internships, 17, 22, 83
intrusive advising, 36, 60, 95, 96, 97

Jahoda, Marie, 34
James, William, 84, 86
Jung, Carl, 9
  on loneliness, 9

K-16 education, 22, 28
Kegan, Robert, 15
Kuh, George, 56, 77, 166

high-impact educational practices, 56–58
iSuccess model will enhance with self-knowledge, 58

LaJambe, Cynthia, 23
locus of control, 8, 85, 86, 89, 127, 135, 139, 140, 148, 156
Lopez, Shane, 93
Lumina Foundation, 15
  study, 15, 16

Magolda, Baxter, 29
Marks, Larry, 33, 34
Maslow, Abraham, 34
meaning in life, 24, 26, 92
mental health, 7
  promotion of positive, 11
mental illness, 7
  paradigm shift to mental health, 34
middle-sized state university, xiii
millennials, 92
mind-body
  causal relationship between, 21, 27
  research, 14, 21
mind-set, xiii, xiv, 5, 9, 11, 15, 20, 47, 58, 70, 78, 79, 101, 106, 108, 152, 158, 159
  new, 15, 27, 31, 44
Minnesota State Colleges and Universities System, 105
motivation, intrinsic, 3, 92
motivations
  external, 19
  internal, 19, 82
  toward dreams and purpose in life, 82

National Academic Advising Association (NACADA), viii
  student success, professional standards, 64–66

National Alliance on Mental Health (2015), 7
National Association of Colleges and Employers (NACE), viii, 75
  student success professional standards, 72
National Association of Student Personnel Administrators (NASPA), viii, 75
  CAPS, 60
  student success professional standards, 58–63
National Career Development Association (NCDA), viii, 75
  student success professional standards, 70–72
National Center for Health Statistics (2106), 7
National Institutes of Health (NIH), 13, 14
  and mind-body research, 14
National Institution of Mental Health (NIMH), 99
National Survey of College Counseling Centers (2014), 6
National Survey of Student Engagement (NSSE), viii, 101, 104, 105
  iSelf and *SAC* adding value to, 105–6
Noncognitive, 34, 52, 57, 74, 135, 151, 152
  factors, 27, 40
  functioning, 34

office of student life
  Ohio State University, The, 50, 144
  University of Michigan, 39
Ohio State University, The, 14, 50, 144
  match between student success mission and practice, 50

Ohio State University (*continued*)
    office of student life, 50
        assessing student wellness, 50
        coordinating numerous departments, 50
        student wellness across the university (counseling and psychological services promising practice), 144
online university, xiii

paradigm, 9
    of life, 9
    of self, 9
    shift from mental illness to mental health, 34
Pennsylvania State University, The, 10, 47, 48, 49, 82, 140, 142, 148, 149
    gap between student success mission and practice, 49
    integrating career counseling and internships using the *iSuccess* model (career counseling high-impact practice), 140–41
    integrating student engagement through university themes (student engagement high-impact practice), 148–50
    Sexual Misconduct Climate Survey (2016), 10
    well-being challenges as representative of all IHEs, 47–48
    WPSU Penn State, 140, 148
personal strengths, 33
positive life course trajectory, 3, 30, 34
positive psychology, 24, 34
    attributes, 90–95
possible selves, 94
posttraumatic stress disorder, 5, 27
potential, 19, 20
    in life, 19
    pathways to, 19
    unique, 19
preventative, 11, 45, 46, 48, 49, 70, 78, 106, 142, 156, 159
    measures, 11
prevention, 8, 11, 12, 13, 28, 44, 45, 46, 47, 52, 60, 70, 100, 109, 145, 155, 159
    through constructing a new self, 47
    well-being education as prevention strategy, 45
professional development, 36–37
    and advantages of using the *iSuccess* model, 36
    for student success professionals, 36
professional standards, student success, xiv
promising practice(s), xiv, xv, 105, 117, 119, 120, 121, 123, 133, 134, 135, 136, 137, 142, 143, 144, 146, 151, 157
    academic advising
        individualized student learning plans (Center for the Self in Schools), 134–35
        online assessments (ePortfolios), 135–36
        workshop series on student success dimensions (University of Michigan), 133
    career counseling
        Designing Your Life Course (Stanford University), 137
        integrating career and academic advising (St. Petersburg), 136–37
    counseling and psychological services (CAPS)
        focus on life purpose (Harvard University), 142
        life coaching and student success coaching (Florida State University), 142–43

online therapy (University of
    Florida), 143–44
student wellness across the
    university (The Ohio State
    University), 144
faculty teaching
    fostering self-direction through
        first-year seminars (Butler
        County Community
        College), 120–21
    student success course
        (Shippensburg University),
        123–27
student engagement
    community engagement (St.
        Petersburg College), 146
    the engaged university (Cornell
        University), 146–47
protective factors, 3, 12, 13, 20, 47, 48, 90
    external, 16
    internal, 16
purpose in life, 5, 25, 26, 27, 78, 79, 84,
    85, 91, 95, 96, 99, 100, 130, 134,
    142, 145, 155, 158
    and lack of, 8

quality of life, xii, 3, 22, 26

real-world learning, 17
relationships, 25
    positive relations with others, 25
Research I university, xiii
resignation, students', 4, 17, 21
resilience, 18
    promoting, 40–41
retention, 16–18, 38
    graduation rates for Latino students,
        39
risk factors, 6, 9, 13, 18, 41, 44
    academic performance, 6
    adjustment to new environment, 6
    anxiety, 6
    depression, 6

family, 6
grief/loss, 6
interpersonal functioning, 6
mood instability, 6
relationship problems, 6
stress, 6
Robinson, Ken, 95
Rogers, Carl, 19, 34
Ryan, Richard, 90, 94
Ryff, Carol, 25–26
    and psychological well-being scales,
        25–26

Scheffler, Israel, 90
self
    acceptance, 26
    affect, 90
    authorship, 38
    concept, 86
    definition of, 26
    destructive behavior, 5
    determination, 25, 94
    development educational
        programming, 46
    discovery, 40
    in education, 26
    efficacy, 87, 102
    esteem, 5, 86
        definition of, 26, 28
        and health, 28
        promotion of, 28
    harm, 5, 21
    inner, 20
    knowledge, xii, xvi, xviii, 2, 5, 12, 13,
        20, 26, 27, 28, 29, 30, 31, 36,
        37, 39, 45, 53, 56, 57, 58, 60,
        61, 66, 67, 68, 69, 70, 72, 74,
        75, 77, 78, 79, 80, 81, 82, 84,
        87, 90 95, 101, 102, 107, 120,
        131, 134, 140, 148, 150, 156,
        157, 158, 159

self-knowledge (*continued*)
   and academic achievement, 27
   in all student success functions, 33
   for the greater good, 79
   lens to view the world, 20
   as part of individual development, 30
   and physical well-being, 27
   and psychological well-being, 27
   responsibility for learning and well-being, 44
   learning through the lens of the, 30
   multidimensional, 27
   referential, 102, 103
   and SAMSHA, 13
   schema, 89
   system attributes, 85–90
   understanding, 18, 87
Self Across the Curriculum (*SAC*), xiv
   and achieving National Survey of Student Engagement results (NSSE), 104
   reflective and integrative learning measures, 104
Seligman, Martin, 24, 90
sexual
   abuse, 28
   assault and violence, 10–11, 45
Shaw, George, Bernard, 91
Shippensburg University of Pennsylvania
   student success course (faculty teaching promising practice), 123–27
Shupp, Matthew
   student success course (Shippensburg University), 123–27
small liberal arts private college, xiii
social and emotional support, 16
social-emotional and cognitive impairment, 27
spirituality, 91
St. Petersburg College, 39, 40, 136, 137, 141, 147
   community engagement (student engagement promising practice), 146
   integrating career and academic advising (career advising promising practice), 136–37
   integrated student success programs, 39
   integrating undergraduate education, career development, and self-discovery, 40
   mission to promote student success, 39
Stanford University
   Designing Your Life Course (career counseling promising practice), 137
Stockton University, 37
strengths-based counseling, 98–101
stress, 81
   management, 45
   students', 5, 6
student affairs, 18, 55
   professional standards, 55
      American College Personnel Association (ACPA), 58–63
   to foster students' integrity and spiritual awareness, 55
   National Association of Student Personnel Administrators (NASPA), 58–63
   to prepare students for careers, citizenship, and lives, 55
student concerns, 6
   academic performance, 6
   adjustment to new environment, 6
   anxiety, 2, 3, 5, 6, 7, 8, 9, 23, 27, 37, 47, 60, 80, 89, 93, 99, 133, 143, 144, 146, 159
   changing needs, 15, 51
   depression, 6
   family, 6
   grief/loss, 6
   interpersonal functioning, 6

Index

mood instability, 6
relationship problems, 6
stress, 6
student development, 20
   changing student development needs, 80
student engagement, xi, 22, 35, 81, 103
   high-impact practices
      integrating student engagement through university themes (The Pennsylvania State University), 148–50
   promising practices
      community engagement (St. Petersburg College), 146
      the engaged university (Cornell University), 146–47
   service learning, 39, 83
   students feeling engaged, 34
student success, xii
   activities, 36
   centers, 41
      Wright State University, 41
   formula, 30
   high-impact practices (*see* high-impact practices)
   individual development as part of, 30
   intellectual growth as part of, 30
   metrics (*see* student success outcomes)
   model (see *Integrated Student Success* model)
   outcomes, 38
   pathways, 30, 33
      personalized pathways to a good life, 30
   professional standards, 55–75
      (*see also* career advising/counseling; counseling and psychological services [CAPS]; faculty teaching; professional standards within academic advising; student affairs)
   redefined, 23–32
   and self-authorship, 38
   students' own definition of, 18
   and well-being, 23
   and wellness, 23–24
student-centered education, 29–30, 38
   and personalized learning plans, 107
   St. Petersburg College's *The College Experience* program, 40
Substance Abuse and Mental Health Services Administration (SAMSHA), 12
   and self-knowledge, 13
Suicide Prevention Resource Center (SPRC), 12
Success Predictor (*SP*), xiv, 78, 80, 108–16
   as assessment instrument, 78
   Figure 5—Structural Tension in High-Impact Student Success Practices, 115
   handbook for administering, 109
   high-impact practice
      aligning life purpose and career using the *Success Predictor* (Center for the Self in Schools), 138
   instructions for advisors, counselors, and faculty, 110, 114
   as intervention instrument, 78
   uses of, 108–9
      academic program interests, 108
      career aspirations, 108
      dreams in life, 108, 109
      formulating a new self, 108–9
      internal motivations to succeed, 108
      internal states of well-being, 108
      purpose in life, 108, 109
suicidal ideation, 7
suicide, 5, 12–13
support services, 17

Ternouth, Andrew, 27
transformation, 81, 98
   of student mind-sets, 78, 99
   of students' lives, 77
   untransformed mind-set, 79
trauma, 5
Twenge, Jean, 2
21st-century, 2, 15, 27, 80
   challenges, 2

University of Central Florida, 33
University of Florida, 143, 144
   online therapy (counseling and psychological services promising practice), 143–44
University of Michigan, 10, 14, 39, 133
   and integrative learning, 39
   office of student life, 39
   workshop series on student success dimensions (academic advising promising practice), 133
University of Pennsylvania, 24, 43–44, 106
   mission to teach students well-being, 43
   student self-responsibility for well-being, 43

Violence Against Women Reauthorization Act (VAWA) (2013), 10

Wade, John, 33, 34, 35
well-being, xi, xii, xiii, 30, 95. *See also* wellness
   in all student success functions, 33
   decline of, 1–22
   education as prevention strategy, 45
   emotional, 27, 146, 152
   and engagement, 25
   gap between prevention and treatment, 44–46
   as guide to prevention and education programs, 52
   high-impact practices to address, 21
   outcomes, 2, 37
   as part of individual development, 30
   physical, 8, 13
      obesity, 8
   promotion of positive, 11
   psychology
      student needs for, 21
      and student success, 23
      in the United States, 7–8
wellness, 23, 24
   Figure 1—A Model of Wellness, 24
   model of, 24
   in society, 32
   and student success, 23
   student wellness holistically, 21
   See also well-being
whole person, 22, 52, 57, 66, 77, 78, 81, 82, 84–85, 96–98, 107, 120, 123, 131, 134, 142, 144, 152, 153, 159
   and advising, 96, 97
   and happiness, 31
   and professional standards
      American College Personnel Association (ACPA), 61
      National Association of Student Personnel Administrators (NASPA), 61
Wilkin, Joshua, 42, 172
   first-year programs and positive psychology, 42
Willoughby, Case, 121, 122
Wright State University
   student success center, 41

Yancy, K. B., 29
Yousafzai, Malala, 15

About the Authors

Henry G. Brzycki, PhD, has more than thirty years of experience providing leadership to the fields of education and psychology. Dr. Brzycki challenges scholars and practitioners to expand their boundaries of understanding in order to impact the quality of people's lives. Dr. Brzycki founded *The Brzycki Group*, where his innovative counseling and psychoeducational programs pioneered positive psychology and strengths-based counseling methods. Dr. Brzycki consults to schools, colleges, foundations, and policy makers on how to realize the potential of people. Most recently, he co-founded *The Center for the Self in Schools*. The Center's nonprofit mission is to impact the psychological, socioemotional, and physical well-being of K-16 students through outreach programs, professional development, self-knowledge curricula, student affairs psychological and career counseling, and student success high-impact practices.

Dr. Brzycki has a distinguished academic and scholarly career, having earned his PhD from The Pennsylvania State University, his MA from Tufts University, and his BS from Babson College. As Dean of the School of Education at American Public University, he transformed teacher and counselor education programs to reflect a visionary 21st century model of education. Dr. Brzycki has provided leadership to the Learning and the Brain Society; the American Counseling Association (ACA); and the American Educational Research Association (AERA), where he has been invited to present his research on numerous occasions. Dr. Brzycki is the author of a bestselling academic book, *The Self in Schooling: Theory and Practice—How to Create Happy, Healthy, Flourishing Children in the 21st Century*, which captures his insights and experiences as a counselor, teacher, and thought leader, and offers a breakthrough model for transforming people's lives, counseling and teaching and learning best practices, and our society.

About the Authors

Elaine J. Brzycki, EdM, serves on the advisory board of *The Brzycki Group*, where she co-develops programs and strategically guides the future of educational services. Ms. Brzycki is co-director of the not-for-profit *Center for The Self in Schools*, leading outreach initiatives. Ms. Brzycki graduated from Wellesley College and attended Oxford University in England. She earned her EdM from the Harvard University Graduate School of Education, and she has over twenty-five years of experience working in higher education, including at Tufts University and Harvard University. Ms. Brzycki is an education strategy and planning manager within WPSU Penn State, a unit of Penn State Outreach and Online Education at The Pennsylvania State University, where she brings to life high-impact projects that require collaboration across multiple university functions and distribution on multiple platforms. She is the former chair of a cross-unit collaboration committee of the Engagement Leadership Team for Penn State Outreach and Online Education, and serves on the Penn State Council on Engaged Scholarship. Her efforts have engaged graduate assistants, student interns, and student volunteers in projects that foster dialog around critical and timely issues in environment, technology, and health. She is committed to empowering people's self-expression and to the transfer of wisdom from one generation to the next.

Related Resources from The Brzycki Group and The Center for the Self in Schools

At the time of publication, the following resources are available. For the most up-to-date information about these resources, please visit www.BrzyckiGroup.com.

1. *Success Predictor* workbooks—Order in paper or online formats, customized with your university's or department's logos or other information.
2. Professional development workshops on the *Integrated Self* (*iSelf*) Model, *Self Across the Curriculum* (*SAC*), and the *Success Predictor* (*SP*)—Participate through face-to-face delivery at your university, or via online meeting platforms.
3. Web-based seminars—Learn methods to help students create good well-being choices and design success pathways; receive handouts, planning sheets, and examples of student-centered applications used in a variety of levels and professional areas of responsibility.
4. Bulk book orders—Order eight or more books and qualify for a 20 percent discount.
5. Social media—Follow updates at our website and on Twitter @ iSelfmodel.
6. Blogging—Submit your articles to us via e-mail for potential posting to our website, or post comments directly to the website to join the conversation.

We always enjoy receiving feedback from professionals and students on your successes; please let us share in your positive lives and the difference you are making. We would also enjoy hearing about your *Success Predictor* hierarchies to see how you are constructing the distinctions and views of success. Share your thoughts via e-mail correspondence: Henry@brzyckigroup.com and Elaine@brzyckigroup.com.

www.ingramcontent.com/pod-product-compliance
Lightning Source LLC
Chambersburg PA
CBHW070943230426
43666CB00011B/2539